Maria Vyasa

KUNDALINI – A BAPTISM OF FIRE

The Journey of the Mystic

AUSTIN MACAULEY PUBLISHERS

LONDON * CAMBRIDGE * NEW YORK * SHARJAH

A CIP catalogue record for this title is available from the British Library.

ISBN 9781035864843 (Paperback)
ISBN 9781035864850 (ePub e-book)

www.austinmacauley.com

First Published 2024
Austin Macauley Publishers Ltd®
1 Canada Square
Canary Wharf
London
E14 5AA

Copyright Notices

Table of Contents

Prologue

The first mystical experience I remember was in a dream as a five-year-old.

A tall lady made of white light, seemingly floating above the floor, came to my bed to wake me up. She said without using her lips to follow her. I felt she was benign so I was not afraid. She took me to a cave. There were others like her there but she was the leader. She 'said' that I was one of them and that I was never alone. They were always with me.

I never forgot the experience. I always carried it with me and felt protected by it.

The mystical experiences never stopped. In my twenties, I learned that the types of experiences I was having were called mystical.

Many people are interested in and impressed by the people having mystical experiences, called the mystics, in different traditions. But they belong to a mystical past and are not expected to exist now.

What seem to be profound truths uttered by those since long gone, may be met with suspicion when uttered in the present.

What is seen as saintly and holy in the past may be seen as too good to be true in the present. Kindness can be seen as

9

a weakness and be taken advantage of. In contrast, people who love power can easily be allowed to wear the robe of holiness.

Also many of the mystic saints in their own time were seen with suspicion, even by the traditions they were part of. Many of them, challenged the hierarchies of their time simply by existing. Some of them were not considered saints until after they had died.

This book is an attempt to understand my life as a mystic through the lens of some mystical traditions.

The traditions I am concentrating on in the book are those that I have worked with and that have deeply affected me; the teachings of Christ and the yogic tradition.

Since Buddha was a part of the yogic tradition as well as a very important developer of that tradition, Buddha is also mentioned as well as the Buddhist Tantras as part of the yogic tradition.

This book does not attempt to be an all-encompassing description of any mystical tradition specifically or of mystical traditions at large.

The Awakening of the Buddha

The texts of Buddha were written about 500 years after his death and most consider them to be symbolical in nature.

Buddha is believed to have lived around 500 BCE. He was a prince in a small kingdom in India. It is said that Buddha, named Siddhartha Gautama, was prevented by his father from encountering any suffering as he grew up. This was because of a prediction made by some seers at Siddhartha's birth. The prediction was that Siddhartha would either become a realized being or a world conqueror. Since the king wanted Siddhartha to inherit his kingdom and make it great, he didn't want Siddhartha to be unsatisfied with the life he lived as a prince but kept him constantly satisfied and undisturbed by anything.

When Siddhartha encounters suffering, this sets him off on a spiritual quest. He realizes the inevitable facts of life that are sickness, old age and death. To find a solution to these, he becomes a wandering seeker.

Siddhartha studies with several teachers/gurus but he still cannot find a solution to the problem of suffering.

He becomes an ascetic and torments the body to purify himself of past karmas and to transcend the body, but as Siddhartha is near death still unrealized, a memory comes back to him. The memory is of him as a child, attending a planting festival with his father. Siddhartha remembers mourning the destruction of the homes of the insects and the death of the small animals in the field, a feeling of compassion and union with all of nature and living beings, and a feeling of happiness and bliss in that.

This experience becomes the turning point for Siddhartha's asceticism. In the legends, it is said that he decides to accept some food after this remembrance. He washes his body for the first time in a long time, and it is said that he puts his begging bowl in the river and asks for it to flow upstream if this is the day he will become enlightened, and it does.

He is then said to have sat down under a Bodhi tree, wowing not to get up until he has reached enlightenment.

As he was sitting there, Mara, the God of death, came to tempt him. He tempted him with what is desirable and tried to scare him with what is not desirable (passion and aversion). The last test Mara subjects Siddhartha to is saying that he, Mara, is the greatest and that all of his armies could attest to that, but that Siddhartha has no one to attest that he is worthy of reaching awakening.

It is said that Siddhartha reached down his hand and touched the earth, and the earth shook.

Mara as the lord of temporal fulfilment and death, rules over the world of men. But Buddha as the awakened one has discovered an order beyond his grasp, an underlying truth that the earth can bear witness to.

It is said that the Buddha awakened after this night of temptation as the morning star (Venus) rose. And he is said to have said, "As the earth is my witness, seeing this morning star, all things and I awaken together."

Buddha wakes up to the true nature of reality and sees the world 'as it is'; yathabhutam. He sees his own and others' previous births, the laws of karma and he is released from the cycle of death and rebirth resulting from karma (samsara).

After Buddha is awakened, he wants to stay in the peace that follows. He also thinks that even if he tried to teach this, no one would understand, or be interested in doing the work required to awaken.

Ayacana Sutta: The request, translation by Thanissaro Bhikku.

Enough now with teaching.
What only with difficulty I reached.
This Dhamma is not easily realised by those overcome with aversion & passion.
What is abstruse, subtle, deep, hard to see, going against the flow—those delighting in passion, cloaked in the mass of darkness, won't see.

It is said that the god Brahma Sahampati comes and begs him to teach what he has learned; his dhamma (Sanskrit: dharma). He says that there are those with a little dust in their eyes, clear enough to understand and to want to do the work. Buddha then agrees to go out to teach.

Ayacana Sutta: The request, translation by Thanissaro Bhikku.

Teach the Dhamma, O Blessed One:
There will be those who will understand.
Then the Blessed One, having understood Brahma's invitation, out of compassion for beings, surveyed the world

13

with the eye of an Awakened One. As he did so, he saw beings with little dust in their eyes and those with much, those with keen faculties and those with dull, those with good attributes and those with bad, those easy to teach and those hard, some of them seeing disgrace and danger in the other world. Just as in a pond of blue or red or white lotuses, some lotuses—born and growing in the water—might flourish while immersed in the water, without rising up from the water; some might stand at an even level with the water; while some might rise up from the water and stand without being smeared by the water—so too, surveying the world with the eye of an Awakened One, the Blessed One saw beings with little dust in their eyes and those with much, those with keen faculties and those with dull, those with good attributes and those with bad, those easy to teach and those hard, some of them seeing disgrace and danger in the other world.

Having seen this, he answered Brahma Sahampati in the verse: Open are the doors to the Deathless to those with ears...

After going out to teach, Buddha first encounters another ascetic. Buddha tells the ascetic that he, Buddha has gone beyond what is deathless and has reached knowledge of the absolute truth. The ascetic asks Buddha for the name of his teacher/guru and Buddha answers that he has reached the state by himself. The ascetic doesn't believe him, and since Buddha has no teacher to testify for him, the ascetic leaves Buddha.

Buddha then goes to teach his former ascetic friends who abandoned him as he accepted the food when he was close to dying. They are said not to want to talk to him at first, but as Buddha claims to have gone beyond, they accept to receive

14

his teaching. After listening to his teaching, they become convinced that he has found a way to experience absolute truth. They become his first students.

The Temptations of Christ

Also, Christ goes through a process of fasting and temptation after his baptism by John the Baptist, when the Spirit of God descends on him.

The baptism can be understood as an act of showing obedience to God. The voice from heaven seems to indicate that Christ is without sin, totally obedient to God.

Matthew 3:13–17 (all quotes from the Bible, New International Version if not stated differently)

Then Jesus came from Galilee to the Jordan to be baptized by John. But John tried to deter him, saying, "I need to be baptized by you, and do you come to me?"

Jesus replied, "Let it be so now; it is proper for us to do this to fulfill all righteousness." Then John consented.

As soon as Jesus was baptized, he went up out of the water. At that moment heaven was opened, and he saw the Spirit of God descending like a dove and alighting on him. And a voice from heaven said, "This is my Son, whom I love; with him I am well pleased."

Fasting probably in both the case of Buddha and Christ is a means of overcoming temptations. Overcoming the temptations marks the start also of Christ's ministry/teaching.

Matthew 4:1–11

Then Jesus was led by the Spirit into the wilderness to be tempted by the devil. After fasting forty days and forty nights, he was hungry. The tempter came to him and said, "If you are the Son of God, tell these stones to become bread."

Jesus answered, "It is written: 'Man shall not live on bread alone, but on every word that comes from the mouth of God'."

Then the devil took him to the holy city and had him stand on the highest point of the temple. "If you are the Son of God," he said, "throw yourself down. For it is written:

'He will command his angels concerning you, and they will lift you up in their hands, so that you will not strike your foot against a stone'."

Jesus answered him, "It is also written: 'Do not put the Lord your God to the test'."

Again, the devil took him to a very high mountain and showed him all the kingdoms of the world and their splendor. "All this I will give you," he said, "if you will bow down and worship me."

Jesus said to him, "Away from me, Satan! For it is written: 'Worship the Lord your God, and serve him only'."

Then the devil left him, and angels came and attended him.

Luke 4:1–13

Jesus, full of the Holy Spirit, left the Jordan and was led by the Spirit into the wilderness, where for forty days he was tempted by the devil. He ate nothing during those days, and at the end of them, he was hungry.

The devil said to him, "If you are the Son of God, tell this stone to become bread."

Jesus answered, "It is written: 'Man shall not live on bread alone'."

The devil led him up to a high place and showed him in an instant all the kingdoms of the world. And he said to him, "I will give you all their authority and splendor; it has been given to me, and I can give it to anyone I want to. If you worship me, it will all be yours."

Jesus answered, "It is written: 'Worship the Lord your God and serve him only'."

The devil led him to Jerusalem and had him stand on the highest point of the temple. "If you are the Son of God," he said, "throw yourself down from here. For it is written:

'He will command his angels concerning you to guard you carefully; they will lift you up in their hands, so that you will not strike your foot against a stone'."

Jesus answered, "It is said: 'Do not put the Lord your God to the test'."

When the devil had finished all this tempting, he left him until an opportune time.

Christ is tempted yet another time in the Bible. This 'opportune time' is the night before the crucifixion.

Matthew 26:36–46

Then Jesus went with his disciples to a place called Gethsemane, and he said to them, "Sit here while I go over

18

there and pray." He took Peter and the two sons of Zebedee along with him, and he began to be sorrowful and troubled. Then he said to them, "My soul is overwhelmed with sorrow to the point of death. Stay here and keep watch with me."

Going a little farther, he fell with his face to the ground and prayed, "My Father, if it is possible, may this cup be taken from me. Yet not as I will, but as you will."

Then he returned to his disciples and found them sleeping. "Couldn't you men keep watch with me for one hour?" he asked Peter. "Watch and pray so that you will not fall into temptation. The spirit is willing, but the flesh is weak."

He went away a second time and prayed, "My Father, if it is not possible for this cup to be taken away unless I drink it, may your will be done."

When he came back, he again found them sleeping, because their eyes were heavy. So he left them and went away once more and prayed the third time, saying the same thing.

Then he returned to the disciples and said to them, "Are you still sleeping and resting? Look, the hour has come, and the Son of Man is delivered into the hands of sinners. Rise! Let us go! Here comes my betrayer!"

In the temptations of Christ, we again as in the case of the Buddha see the themes of passion (hunger), aversion (avoidance of suffering) and power (desire for power).

These temptations are the same as the temptations given in the three lowest chakras given below, as proposed these may be connected to the last three of the Mahavidyas also given below.

Deathlessness

There is a clear indication of a process of death and resurrection in the awakening story of Buddha. This can be seen in the almost death from asceticism practice of starvation that leads up to the realization of Buddha, and the symbology of the morning star rising as Buddha awakens. Buddha is also sometimes described as filling up and getting a radiant complexion after eating his first meal after breaking the fast.

This process of death and resurrection, as well as the morning star as a symbol of this process, is already found in the ancient Sumerian myth of Inanna.

In this myth, Goddess Inanna goes through a death and resurrection process. Inanna is deeply connected with the planet Venus and the change that Venus goes through in its cycle.

Since Venus disappears from the sky in its change from morning star to evening star (and reverse) and then reappears, it has since ancient times been seen as connected to a process of death and resurrection.

The light of Venus as the morning star also heralds the sun and because of this, it is associated with the return of life.

The story of Inanna is about conquering death and escaping the birth and death cycle. Inanna is killed by her sister Ereshkigal, the goddess of the life and death cycle. In the end, she is resurrected and her husband and his sister, symbols for vegetation, livestock and fertility, take her place in the birth-death cycle.

It becomes clear in the story that Innana receives the power; 'the me', of the underworld, and although you cannot leave the underworld with that 'me', Inanna does, as she is resurrected. Maybe this points out that the underworld/death no longer has any power over her.

Also in the story of Buddha, there is a theme of 'death of death' or the defeat of death. Mara who tried to hinder Buddha from awakening is the God of death and therefore over all that is under the laws of change. Buddha resisting the temptations over what is temporal, gains the state of what is beyond change, what is absolute, unchanging and undying. He is said to have reached a deathless state. This is a new form of existence as is indicated by the rising of the morning star and the dawning of a new day after a night of temptation.

It is not difficult to see the same themes in the story of Christ; Christ's night of trial and agony in the face of death before the crucifixion and the resurrection after death into a deathless state.

In both the story of Buddha and the story of Christ, the connection to the material world is clear. This is the reason why the representations of temporal fulfilment and death, the devil and Mara, are trying to stop them. Buddha and Christ are going beyond their realm of power, but this going beyond is not happening solely in some other realm, but influencing the material world.

As Buddha touches the ground to ask the earth to be his witness for being awakened, it is said that the earth shook in response. Christ is resurrected with his body. It is said that when he died, the heaven became dark as night and the veil in the temple was torn from top to bottom. Christ sends the Holy Spirit to his disciples to be with them and work through them (performing miracles) when he is gone. Both Buddha and Christ perform miracles in their own lives.

The stories are clear. The deathless state has the power to change the material world. It is a higher order.

Prakasha-Ohr Ein Sof-Kingdom of Heaven

In the tantric school of Pratyabhijna (ca 900 CE) is presented the idea of Prakasha, which is the light of being and consciousness that all is part of. This is also called 'the void' but must not be understood as an empty space but rather as an ocean of light or potential energy pulsating, says the religious scholar oriented towards Classical Tantra and Sanskritist Christopher Wallis. This idea of the Prakasha is of course built on other more ancient ideas in Indian philosophy.

The oldest hymn of something divine in India is the Saivitri (Gayatri) mantra.

Om bhur bhuvah svah tat savitur varenyam bhargo devasya dheemahi dhiyo yo nah prachodayaat.

Om. We worship Saivitur (who is all of the three worlds). We ask that its light may enlighten our intellects (approximately translated).

This hymn is from the oldest of the Rig Vedas, the third book, from around 1500 BCE. The part with the three worlds is added on later in 800 BCE.

This is understood as a hymn to the sun, but as we see the understanding of the sun as something that can illumine the human intellect gives it a more symbolic meaning than we usually give to the physical sun in modern times.

Elaine Pagels, professor of religion, points out that the first emanation leading to the creation of the Hebrew God according to Genesis was a light. Not the light of the sun, moon or stars because they were created later, but some form of primordial light.

The prophets of the Jewish tradition also often describe God as light. Moses hears God in a bush that seems to be burning but does not burn up. The prophet Ezekiel sees the likeness of God as different forms of light and radiance.

Elaine Pagels brings up the saying in Genesis that God created humans in the image of God and what that can mean in a tradition that doesn't allow for representations of God. She proposes that it might be the light that is referred to.

Jewish mysticism Kabbalah talks about a divine light that emanated from God at the time of creation as 'Ohr Ein Sof'.

Also in the New Testament, the idea of the light of God is present.

John 8:12

When Jesus spoke again to the people, he said, "I am the light of the world.
Whoever follows me will never walk in darkness, but will have the light of life."

It is clear that Christ speaks here of himself in connection to God by the continuation.

John 8:19

Then they asked him, "Where is your father?"
"You do not know me or my Father," Jesus replied. "If
you knew me, you would know my Father also."

There is also a visual expression of the light of Christ in
the story of the transfiguration of Christ at Mount Tabor.

Matthew 17:1–3

After six days, Jesus took with him Peter, James and John,
the brother of James, and led them up a high mountain by
themselves. There he was transfigured before them. His face
shone like the sun, and his clothes became as white as the
light. Just then there appeared before them Moses and Elijah,
talking with Jesus.

But is it only Jesus that is the light of God?

Matthew 5:14–16

You are the light of the world. A town built on a hill cannot
be hidden. Neither do people light a lamp and put it under a
bowl. Instead, they put it on its stand, and it gives light to
everyone in the house. In the same way, let your light shine
before others, that they may see your good deeds and glorify
your Father in heaven.

Some of the gospels talk about the kingdom of heaven as
a place, a state of being after death, or a new order on earth.

Elaine Pagels thinks that this is because the followers of Christ interpreted the message of Christ, that the kingdom was close, in different ways.

One way that it is described is found in the gospel of Luke.

Luke 17:21

nor will people say, 'Here it is,' or 'There it is,' because the kingdom of God is in your midst."

The wording here translated as 'in your midst' can also be translated as within or among you.

In texts found at Nag Hammadi in 1945, developments of concepts found in the New Testament are found. Elaine Pagels has made the Nag Hammadi texts her life work.

One of the Nag Hammadi texts is the Gospel of Thomas. Most researchers believe this text to be a compilation of early documentation of the sayings of Christ mixed with later material.

This text has sayings found in the canonical gospels but sometimes has added meaning to what is not explained in the sayings of the canonical gospels. The text proclaims itself to be the secret teachings of Jesus.

That Christ may have had a secret teaching is indicated in one of the canonical gospels (see below). It would also be in accordance with how rabbis/religious teachers taught at the time, giving one teaching in public and another to the more initiated, according to Elaine Pagels.

Mark 4:10–12

When he was alone, the Twelve and the others around him asked him about the parables. He told them, "The secret of the kingdom of God has been given to you. But to those on the outside everything is said in parables so that,

'they may be ever seeing but never perceiving and ever hearing but never understanding; otherwise, they might turn and be forgiven'!"

Gospel of Thomas, translation by Stephen Patterson and Marvin Meyer

Logion 3

Jesus said, "If your leaders say to you, 'Look, the (Father's) kingdom is in the sky,' then the birds of the sky will precede you. If they say to you, 'It is in the sea,' then the fish will precede you. Rather, the (Father's) kingdom is within you and it is outside you.

When you know yourselves, then you will be known, and you will understand that you are children of the living Father. But if you do not know yourselves, then you live in poverty, and you are the poverty."

So what does this text imply is what is inside us and among us?

Logion 77

Jesus said, "I am the light that is over all things. I am all: from me, all came forth, and to me all attained.
Split a piece of wood; I am there.
Lift up the stone, and you will find me there."

Logion 24

His disciples said, "Show us the place where you are, for we must seek it."

He said to them, "Anyone here with two ears had better listen! There is light within a person of light, and it shines on the whole world. If it does not shine, it is dark."

What sort of light is this, and what is its origin?

Logion 50

Jesus said, "If they say to you, 'Where have you come from?' say to them, 'We have come from the light, from the place where the light came into being by itself, established [itself], and appeared in their image.'
If they say to you, 'Is it you?' say, 'We are its children, and we are the chosen of the living Father.'
If they ask you, 'What is the evidence of your Father in you?' say to them, 'It is motion and rest'."

Elaine Pagels believes this verse refers to Genesis, where the light came into being by itself, and in God's image created humankind. Also, the reference to motion and rest can be traced to the motion and rest of God in the creation of the world in Genesis.

In another of the Nag Hammadi gospels; "The Gospel of Truth," translation by Robert M. Grant, it says:

Say then in your heart that you are this perfect day and that in you the light which does not fail dwells.

Truth

As we have seen, Buddha wakes up to the true nature of reality.

He realizes the difficulty of teaching what he has discovered since people are overcome by aversion and passion and the teaching is subtle and going against the flow.

He also realizes that there are those with little dust in their eyes who can understand the teaching and who can be willing to follow it.

This is talking about a capacity to see clearly, to recognize truth and to want to follow truth.

When questioned by Pilate, Christ is asked if he is the king of the Jews. Christ answers that his kingdom is not of this world.

John 18:37–38

"You are a king, then!" said Pilate.

Jesus answered, "You say that I am a king. In fact, the reason I was born and came into the world is to testify to the truth. Everyone on the side of truth listens to me."

"What is truth?" retorted Pilate…

In this conversation, two very important things are said.

First, Christ explains that the reason he was born was to bear witness to the truth. This truth also seems connected to the kingdom of God.

Second, Pilate answers to this 'What is truth?' seeming to dismiss the existence of such a thing.

We still have this problem today. We talk about the relativity of truth, the subjectivity of truth, about truth as a collective enterprise uniting different perspectives to get a bigger picture that still never can become complete.

But the absolute truth that Buddha and Christ talked about is still questioned.

Our relationship to truth is still a collective enterprise of finding support for our claims.

We also have the method of objective observation, testing and retesting to see if we get the same results each time.

So what does Christ mean by saying that he bears witness to the truth?

John 8:12–18

When Jesus spoke again to the people, he said, "I am the light of the world. Whoever follows me will never walk in darkness, but will have the light of life."

The Pharisees challenged him, "Here you are, appearing as your own witness; your testimony is not valid."

Jesus answered, "Even if I testify on my own behalf, my testimony is valid, for I know where I came from and where I am going. But you have no idea where I come from or where I am going. You judge by human standards; I pass judgment on no one. But if I do judge, my decisions are true, because I am not alone. I stand with the Father, who sent me. In your own Law, it is written that the testimony of two witnesses is true. I am one who testifies for myself; my other witness is the Father, who sent me."

John 5:31–43

"If I testify about myself, my testimony is not true. There is another who testifies in my favor, and I know that his testimony about me is true.

You have sent to John and he has testified to the truth. Not that I accept human testimony; but I mention it that you may be saved. John was a lamp that burned and gave light, and you chose for a time to enjoy his light."

"I have testimony weightier than that of John. For the works that the Father has given me to finish—the very works that I am doing—testify that the Father has sent me. And the Father who sent me has himself testified concerning me. You have never heard his voice nor seen his form, nor does his word dwell in you, for you do not believe the one he sent. You study the Scriptures diligently because you think that in them you have eternal life. These are the very Scriptures that testify about me, yet you refuse to come to me to have life."

"I do not accept glory from human beings, but I know you. I know that you do not have the love of God in your hearts. I have come in my Father's name, and you do not accept me; but if someone else comes in his own name, you will accept him.

Here we see that Christ finds the human ways of testing truth by means of a collective agreement and human authority as inadequate.

The same theme, as we have seen, is found in the story of Buddha's encounter with the ascetic after his awakening. In the story, the ascetic asks Buddha for the name of his teacher/guru. When Buddha explains that he has reached the awakened state on his own, the ascetic is not interested in listening but leaves Buddha.

Christ also shows how arbitrary the human distinction between true and false is.

John 15:22–24

If I had not come and spoken to them, they would not be guilty of sin; but now they have no excuse for their sin. Whoever hates me hates my Father as well. If I had not done among them the works no one else did, they would not be guilty of sin. As it is, they have seen, and yet they have hated both me and my Father.

John 8:42–47

Jesus said to them, "If God were your Father, you would love me, for I have come here from God. I have not come on my own; God sent me. Why is my language not clear to you? Because you are unable to hear what I say. You belong to your father, the devil, and you want to carry out your father's desires. He was a murderer from the beginning, not holding to the truth, for there is no truth in him. When he lies, he speaks his native language, for he is a liar and the father of

33

lies. Yet because I tell the truth, you do not believe me! Can any of you prove me guilty of sin? If I am telling the truth, why don't you believe me? Whoever belongs to God hears what God says. The reason you do not hear is that you do not belong to God."

Then what about the scientific way of testing and retesting?

Matthew 8:1–4

When Jesus came down from the mountainside, large crowds followed him. A man with leprosy came and knelt before him and said, "Lord, if you are willing, you can make me clean."

Jesus reached out his hand and touched the man. "I am willing," he said. "Be clean!"

Immediately he was cleansed of his leprosy.

Then Jesus said to him, "See that you don't tell anyone. But go, show yourself to the priest and offer the gift Moses commanded, as a testimony to them."

Luke 17:11–14

Now on his way to Jerusalem, Jesus travelled along the border between Samaria and Galilee. As he was going into a village, ten men who had leprosy met him. They stood at a distance and called out in a loud voice, "Jesus, Master, have pity on us!"

When he saw them, he said, "Go, show yourselves to the priests." And as they went, they were cleansed.

In both of these stories, Jesus is clear about one of the functions of the miracles. This is to be testimony/evidence of truth. He is showing that what he says is true by his miracles, and he repeats these miracles many times as a testimony to this truth.

The truth seems to be that there is a law above the laws of humans and the transient world, and Christ is in contact with that truth, which is God.

This higher order of truth is also connected to life.

John 11:38–45

Jesus, once more deeply moved, came to the tomb. It was a cave with a stone laid across the entrance. "Take away the stone," he said.

"But, Lord," said Martha, the sister of the dead man, "by this time there is a bad odor, for he has been there four days."

Then Jesus said, "Did I not tell you that if you believe, you will see the glory of God?"

So they took away the stone. Then Jesus looked up and said, "Father, I thank you that you have heard me. I knew that you always hear me, but I said this for the benefit of the people standing here, that they may believe that you sent me."

When he had said this, Jesus called in a loud voice, "Lazarus, come out!" The dead man came out, his hands and feet wrapped with strips of linen, and a cloth around his face.

Jesus said to them, "Take off the grave clothes and let him go."

The higher order of truth is not only connected to life but to eternal life.

John 17:3

*Now this is eternal life: that they know you, the only true
God, and Jesus Christ, whom you have sent.*

What then can be said about the nature of truth? The
Gospel of Truth, one of the Nag Hammadi Gospels talks about
this.

Gospel of Truth, translation by Robert M. Grant.

*For this reason, do not take error too seriously. Thus,
since it had no root, it was in u fog as regards the Father,
engaged in preparing works and forgetfulnesses and fears in
order, by these means, to beguile those of the middle and to
make them captive.*

*He revealed himself as a Pleroma, i.e., the finding of the
light of truth which has shined towards him, because he is
unchangeable.*

The last passage talks about Christ.

Here we can see 'error' described as without root. This
reminds us of the idea of maya, meaning illusion in the Vedic
and Buddhist contexts. Illusion is always described as
inherently weak, as it lacks existential ground.

The search for truth must therefore be the search for what
is consistent and unchanging.

It will be of a higher order than that which is illusory.

Jesus shows his connection to the truth through his
teaching and his miracles. They are proof of a higher order of
truth. This order is of deathlessness and eternal life.

Jesus often talks of this order of life as opposed to sin which gives sickness and death.

Matthew 9:1–8

Jesus stepped into a boat, crossed over and came to his own town. Some men brought to him a paralyzed man, lying on a mat. When Jesus saw their faith, he said to the man, "Take heart, son; your sins are forgiven."

At this, some of the teachers of the law said to themselves, "This fellow is blaspheming!"

Knowing their thoughts, Jesus said, "Why do you entertain evil thoughts in your hearts? Which is easier: to say, 'Your sins are forgiven,' or to say, 'Get up and walk'? But I want you to know that the Son of Man has authority on earth to forgive sins." So he said to the paralyzed man, "Get up, take your mat and go home'." Then the man got up and went home. When the crowd saw this, they were filled with awe; and they praised God, who had given such authority to man.

John 5:24

"Very truly I tell you, whoever hears my word and believes him who sent me has eternal life and will not be judged but has crossed over from death to life.

Christ also talks about truth as freedom.

John 8:31–34

To the Jews who had believed him, Jesus said, "If you hold to my teaching, you are really my disciples. Then you will know the truth, and the truth will set you free."

They answered him, "We are Abraham's descendants and have never been slaves of anyone. How can you say that we shall be set free?"

Jesus replied, "Very truly I tell you, everyone who sins is a slave to sin.

Christ says that the world neither sees, knows nor accepts the Spirit of truth. Only the eyes of the living that are in contact with truth can see at this level of truth. The truth is therefore connected to life.

John 14:15–21

"If you love me, keep my commands. And I will ask the Father, and he will give you another advocate to help you and be with you forever—the Spirit of truth. The world cannot accept him, because it neither sees him nor knows him. But you know him, for he lives with you and will be in you. I will not leave you as orphans; I will come to you. Before long, the world will not see me anymore, but you will see me. Because I live, you also will live. On that day, you will realize that I am in my Father, and you are in me, and I am in you. Whoever has my commands and keeps them is the one who loves me. The one who loves me will be loved by my Father, and I too will love them and show myself to them."

Here in this last speech to the disciples, Christ also explains the reason why Christ must be crucified. It is not because the laws of the world have any hold on him. It is proof of the unrestricted love and obedience of Christ to the Father.

John 14:30–31

I will not say much more to you, for the prince of this world is coming. He has no hold over me, but he comes so that the world may learn that I love the Father and do exactly what my Father has commanded me.

Come now; let us leave.

As we have seen in the temptations of Christ, 'the prince of the world' (compare with Buddha and Mara; god of death) has no hold over him.

Christ talks about condemnation and the falsehood of the world. He also brings up the reason why people don't want to accept the truth.

John 16:11

and about judgment, because the prince of this world now stands condemned.

John 3:19–21

This is the verdict: Light has come into the world, but people loved darkness instead of light because their deeds were evil. Everyone who does evil hates the light, and will not come into the light for fear that their deeds will be exposed.

But whoever lives by the truth comes into the light, so that it may be seen plainly that what they have done has been done in the sight of God.

Here again, we see the connection in the teaching of Christ between the truth, the light, seeing things clearly as well as having nothing to hide.

Also, the subject of evil is brought up here, connected to the notion of sin, both of which we will discuss later.

Baptism in Water and Fire

The Bible talks about a baptism with water as repentance for the forgiveness of sins, performed by John the Baptist. But there is also another form of baptism mentioned in the Bible performed by Christ, a baptism with Holy Spirit and fire.

Mark 1:4–8

And so John the Baptist appeared in the wilderness, preaching a baptism of repentance for the forgiveness of sins. The whole Judean countryside and all the people of Jerusalem went out to him. Confessing their sins, they were baptized by him in the Jordan River. John wore clothing made of camel's hair, with a leather belt around his waist, and he ate locusts and wild honey. And this was his message: "After me comes the one more powerful than I, the straps of whose sandals I am not worthy to stoop down and untie. I baptize you with water, but he will baptize you with the Holy Spirit."

Matthew 3:11–12

"I baptize you with water for repentance. But after me comes one who is more powerful than I, whose sandals I am

not worthy to carry. He will baptize you with the Holy Spirit and fire. His winnowing fork is in his hand, and he will clear his threshing floor, gathering his wheat into the barn and burning up the chaff with unquenchable fire."

The Gospel of Thomas, Translated by Thomas O. Lambdin.

Logion 82

Jesus said, "He who is near me is near the fire, and he who is far from me is far from the kingdom."

Jesus explains that two births are necessary to enter the kingdom of God. Here the birth of water seems connected to human birth. It also talks of a birth in Spirit.

John 3:5–7

Jesus answered, "Very truly, I tell you, no one can enter the kingdom of God unless they are born of water and the Spirit. Flesh gives birth to flesh, but the Spirit gives birth to spirit. You should not be surprised at my saying, 'You must be born again.'

The baptism with Holy Spirit is as we have seen connected to fire.

The image of fire is very popular to describe God and God's angels in the Bible.

Hebrews 12:29

for our "God is a consuming fire."

Exodus 3:2

There the angel of the LORD appeared to him in flames of fire from within a bush. Moses saw that though the bush was on fire it did not burn up.

Ezekiel 1:25–28

Then there came a voice from above the vault over their heads as they stood with lowered wings. Above the vault over their heads was what looked like a throne of lapis lazuli, and high above on the throne was a figure like that of a man. I saw that from what appeared to be his waist up he looked like glowing metal, as if full of fire, and that from there down he looked like fire; and brilliant light surrounded him. Like the appearance of a rainbow in the clouds on a rainy day, so was the radiance around him.

This was the appearance of the likeness of the glory of the lord. When I saw it, I fell facedown, and I heard the voice of one speaking.

God is also spoken about as Spirit in the New Testament.

John 4:24

God is spirit, and his worshipers must worship in the Spirit and in truth."

Christ talks about his work on earth as kindling fire. He also talks about his crucifixion and death as a baptism.

Luke 12:49–51

"I have come to bring fire on the earth, and how I wish it were already kindled! But I have a baptism to undergo, and what constraint I am under until it is completed! Do you think I came to bring peace on earth? No, I tell you, but division.

He refers to the work that God gave him to do; to give eternal life to those God gave him, by knowing God.

John 17:1–5

After Jesus said this, he looked toward heaven and prayed:

"Father, the hour has come. Glorify your Son, that your Son may glorify you. For you granted him authority over all people that he might give eternal life to all those you have given him. Now this is eternal life: that they know you, the only true God, and Jesus Christ, whom you have sent. I have brought you glory on earth by finishing the work you gave me to do. And now, Father, glorify me in your presence with the glory I had with you before the world began.

This baptism of Christ seems to be to conquer 'the prince of the world' for the possible liberation of all into eternal life.

John 12:27–32

"Now my soul is troubled, and what shall I say? 'Father, save me from this hour'? No, it was for this very reason I came to this hour. Father, glorify your name!"

Then a voice came from heaven, "I have glorified it, and will glorify it again." The crowd that was there and heard it said it had thundered; others said an angel had spoken to him.

Jesus said, "This voice was for your benefit, not mine. Now is the time for judgment on this world; now the prince of this world will be driven out. And I, when I am lifted up from the earth, will draw all people to myself."

John 11:25–26

... I am the resurrection and the life. The one who believes in me will live, even though they die; and whoever lives by believing in me will never die...

The crucifixion of Christ seems to be a conquering of death (prince of the world), not for Christ but for the benefit of everyone willing to receive. This is similar to the idea of the Buddha and the Bodhisattva in Buddhism.

When it comes to people in general the baptism in fire and Spirit seems to refer to a personal process of becoming into Spirit, a glorification.

Romans 8:28–30

And we know that in all things God works for the good of those who love him, who have been called according to his purpose. For those God foreknew he also predestined to be conformed to the image of his Son, that he might be the firstborn among many brothers and sisters. And those he predestined, he also called; those he called, he also justified; those he justified, he also glorified.

The glorification seems to follow the process of becoming righteous/justified. Righteousness is also central in the Vedic tradition as dharma and is also here an expression of the quality of the divine. Righteousness seems to be an expression of truth, life and unity.

The word 'glory' (Hebrew; kavod, Greek; doxa) refers to the light and splendor which is the essential expression of God.

Exodus 33:18–20

Then Moses said, "Now show me your glory."
And the LORD said, "I will cause all my goodness to pass in front of you, and I will proclaim my name, the LORD, in your presence. I will have mercy on whom I will have mercy, and I will have compassion on whom I will have compassion. But," he said, "you cannot see my face, for no one may see me and live."

Exodus 34:29

When Moses came down from Mount Sinai with the two tablets of the covenant law in his hands, he was not aware that his face was radiant because he had spoken with the LORD.

2 Corinthians 3:17–18

Now the Lord is the Spirit, and where the Spirit of the Lord is, there is freedom. And we all, who with unveiled faces contemplate the Lord's glory, are being transformed into his image with ever-increasing glory, which comes from the Lord, who is the Spirit.

In the transfiguration of Jesus at Mount Tabor, his disciples saw Christ's glory.

Matthew 17:1–3

After six days, Jesus took with him Peter, James and John the brother of James, and led them up a high mountain by themselves. There he was transfigured before them. His face shone like the sun, and his clothes became as white as the light. Just then there appeared before them Moses and Elijah, talking with Jesus.

Glory seems to be connected to unity.

John 17:22-23

I have given them the glory that you gave me, that they may be one as we are one—I in them and you in me—so that they may be brought to complete unity…

In one of the Nag Hammadi gospels 'Gospel of Truth', we find a unification process described as a fire devouring matter, light devouring darkness and life devouring death.

Gospel of Truth, translation by Robert M. Grant

By means of unity each one will understand itself. By means of knowledge, it will purify itself of diversity with a view towards unity, devouring matter within itself like fire and darkness by light, death by life.

In another of the Nag Hammadi gospels 'Gospel of Philip', the soul and the spirit are said to come into being from fire and water (like the baptisms).

Gospel of Philip, translation by Wesley W. Isenberg

It is from water and fire that the soul and the spirit came into being. It is from water and fire and light that the son of the bridal chamber (came into being). The fire is the chrism, the light is the fire. I am not referring to that fire which has no form, but to the other fire whose form is white, which is bright and beautiful, and which gives beauty.

Further, this glorification seems to be a return to the condition before and after the creation, an underlying condition.

Gospel of Thomas, translation by Stephen Patterson and Marvin Meyer

Logion 50

Jesus said, "If they say to you, 'Where have you come from?' say to them, 'We have come from the light, from the

place where the light came into being by itself, established [itself], and appeared in their image.'

If they say to you, 'Is it you?' say, 'We are its children, and we are the chosen of the living Father.'

If they ask you, 'What is the evidence of your Father in you?' say to them, 'It is motion and rest'."

John 17:5

And now, Father, glorify me in your presence with the glory I had with you before the world began.

Gospel of Thomas, translation by Thomas O. Lambdin

Logion 18

The disciples said to Jesus, "Tell us how our end will be."

Jesus said, "Have you discovered, then, the beginning, that you look for the end? For where the beginning is, there will the end be. Blessed is he who will take his place in the beginning; he will know the end and will not experience death."

Logion 19

Jesus said, "Blessed is he who came into being before he came into being. If you become my disciples and listen to my words, these stones will minister to you. For there are five trees for you in Paradise, which remain undisturbed summer and winter and whose leaves do not fall. Whoever becomes acquainted with them will not experience death."

The Five Wisdom Qualities in Buddhist Tantra

The five wisdom Buddhas (Pancha Tathagatas) are a development of the Buddhist Tantras.

They are Akshobhya, Ratnasambhava, Vairocana, Amitabha and Amoghasiddhi.

The five Buddhas are aspects of the dharmakaya; dharma-body, which embodies the principles of awakeness in Buddhism.

The five wisdom qualities in the Buddhist Vajrayana according to Robert Thurman, professor of Indo-Tibetan Buddhist studies are accordingly:

The white wisdom quality is mirror-like wisdom. It transforms delusion into truth. It is also connected to lightning.

The red wisdom quality transforms desire and greed into individuated appreciation.

The golden wisdom is the wisdom of equality. It transforms pride and stinginess into the understanding that everything is of equal value.

The green wisdom quality is the transformation of envy, which is a mixture of hate and desire, into the wisdom of miracle-working and omnipresence.

The dark blue wisdom quality is the transformation of hatred, connected to the analytical, intellectual understanding that comes by taking things apart, into the ultimate reality of perfection which is the understanding of the infinite presence of clear light also in immanence. It is a luminous darkness that exists at the threshold of transparency.

The white wisdom quality is a form of diamond plasma energy.

The red wisdom quality is a form of ruby plasma energy.

The golden wisdom quality is a form of yellow sapphire plasma energy.

The green wisdom quality is a form of emerald plasma energy.

The dark blue wisdom quality is a form of sapphire plasma energy.

The void (shunyata) that is nirvana in this tradition is a realm of infinite diamond-like light of infinite energy. This is the absolute, meaning unchanging, truth. This is similar to the 'Prakasha' of the Pratyabijna school.

The idea of wisdom qualities in the form of divine light of different colors is also found in the Jewish mystic school of Kabbalah as the Sefirot.

In the Hindu Shakta Tantra, we can find similar wisdom qualities in the form of some of the Dasa (ten) Mahavidyas.

The dark blue as well as the white wisdom quality has the form of the goddess Tara in this system. Tara is the bridge between the unmanifest and the manifest. She is connected to the slightly lit-up dark blue sky, the color dark blue or blue-black. Her name Tara can be understood as 'star' and as such she is connected to a clear diamond-like light. As a bridge between manifest and unmanifest, she also represents transcendence in immanence. Immanence is the transcendent divided by maya into multiplicity in the tantric cosmology.

The goddess Tara is believed to have originated from Buddhist Tantra. The word Tara means 'the savior' or 'the liberator'. Her name originates from the Sanskrit root 'tr', meaning 'passing over'. In Buddhist Tantra, she is said to take one across/beyond samsara (the cycle of birth-death-rebirth). Tara is said to transform delusion into truth.

The red wisdom quality has the form of Tripurasundari. Tripurasundari symbolizes the impulse of desire and will (iccha shakti) in its form as the erotic impulse, but also the ability to turn that desire and will towards the divine (from the root-div, in Sanskrit meaning shining). She also symbolizes the ability to enjoy the individuated (divided) expression of the divine, as manifested. This fits well with transforming desire and greed into individuated appreciation.

The golden wisdom quality has the form of Bhagalamukhi. She is connected to the quality of arrest, and by that to the central channel (Shushumna) and the ending of Ida and Pingala representing a life of polarities controlled by aversion and desire. This fits well with the realization that everything is of equal value. The vayu (life force) is seemingly connected to Bhagalamuki; Samana is an equalising form of life force that draws all energies together and takes them back in the form of Kundalini to an undivided state.

The green wisdom quality has the form of Matangi. Matangi symbolizes transcending the desire for power. This fits well with the transformation of envy since envy is ruled by the desire for power. The transformation of envy into miracle-working and omnipresence can be understood as the result of anava-mala, the experience of separation, being destroyed. It is only in the experience of separation that one can experience envy. Miracle works and omnipresence can only be possible in an unseparated state.

If my analysis is correct, Matangi may also be connected to the Svadhistana chakra (read more below). It is said that Svadhistana (connected to desire) dissolves jealousy in its waters as it awakens.

Dasa Mahavidyas-The Ten Wisdom Qualities in Hindu Tantra

According to David Kinsley, professor of religion, the ten (dasa) Mahavidyas were known as a group since the early medieval period (after the tenth century CE).

The Mahavidyas are tantric in origin and incorporate goddesses from different lineages of Tantra.

Many believe that the Mahavidyas are symbols of the Kundalini process. We will see through this symbology and later explanation of the Kundalini process that the Kundalini process is a downward trajectory into creation, an upward trajectory into liberation and a downward trajectory as an expression of that liberation.

The Mahavidyas are: Kali, Tara, Tripurasundari, Bhuvaneshvari, Bhairavi, Chinnamasta, Dhumavati, Bhagalamukhi, Matangi and Kamala.

This order is not always given. Sometimes there are also given more than ten (dasa) Mahavidyas.

There is only one academic book written on the Mahavidyas in English, *Tantric Visions of the Divine Feminine: The Ten Mahavidyas* by David Kinsley.

There are also two informative non-academic books written on the topic by Sally Kempton, *Awakening Shakti* and by Kavitha M. Chinnaiyan, *Shakti Rising*, both practitioners in tantric traditions.

These books are the base of the knowledge given below.

Some of the ideas presented here are my own and informed by my experiences. These are presented as propositions so that they may not be read as conclusions from academic research or informed by the living tantric traditions mentioned above.

Kali

The name Kali means 'the black one'.

In the Mahanirvanatantra Shiva praises Kali as 'she who devours time,' and who is the destroyer and origin of all things. As such, she is both the dissolution of the world (pralaya) and the primordial shakti (adi shakti). This is why Kali is the first of the Mahavidyas.

Her black color is said to symbolize her transcendence of all forms (nirguna).

She might also be connected to darkness because she is the 'jagad yoni' (the womb of the universe) from where everything comes and returns.

Maybe the darkness also symbolizes the gate to the unknown. In many religious traditions, God is explained as beyond our grasp of knowing.

In her nirguna form (without form), she seems to be symbolizing the void state (nothingness) beyond creation.

In the chakra system, the void is associated with Sahasrara (the crown lotus).

David Kinsley proposes that Kali's nudity represents totally illuminated consciousness, unaffected by maya, as a fire of truth that burns away all that is not in accordance with it (compare with baptism of fire and Kundalini).

A religious scholar specializing in Tantra and Sanskritist, Christopher Wallis has found in a text from the Trika school of Tantra, a 700-century text called 'Siddhi Yogeshwari Mata' Kundalini described as 'jagad yoni.' This is according to Wallis the first mention of Kundalini in any found scripture. Here Kundalini is described as 'jagad yoni' (the womb of the universe) and as the source of all the Sanskrit letters.

Kali is said to be the source of the Sanskrit letters as the underlying essence of reality preceding and underlying the sound; OM.

The garland of heads around Kali's neck is said to represent all the letters of the Sanskrit alphabet. Since the universe is said to be ultimately sonic in its nature in this system, this means she is what underlies all of creation.

This position of being the beginning of all creation has lent Kali the position of Adi Shakti; the primal power in the Mahavidya system. In the origin myths of Dasa Mahavidyas, Kali is also the first to manifest.

Kali might be identified with Bindu in the chakra system, a point of infinitely concentrated energy from where all of the multitude of creation is created or returns to the source.

Tara

Tara is the bridge between the unmanifest and the manifest. She is connected to the slightly lit-up dark blue sky, the color dark blue or blue-black and a transparent white star or brilliant radiance.

The word Tara means 'the savior' or 'the liberator'. Her name originates from the Sanskrit root 'tr', meaning 'passing over'. In Buddhist Tantra, she is said to take one across/beyond samsara (the cycle of birth-death-rebirth). Another meaning of her name is star, according to Kavitha Chinnaiyan, a practitioner of the tantric Sri Vidya tradition and author.

Tara is the first sonic vibration of manifestation, in the Vedas explained to be OM.

OM is said to densify into the elements of creation, which makes Tara the first emanation of creative force. OM is written inside the lotus of the visualization of the Ajna chakra.

As the first manifestation of creative force, Tara might be identified as the first emanation from the Bindu into creation (see 'Chakras').

The union of Shiva (underlying unchanging light) and Shakti (the projection of that source of light, as different manifestations) also happens in Bindu.

Bindu is a point of infinitely concentrated energy from where all of the multitude of creation is created or returns to the source.

As creation takes place, the Bindu explodes generating the universe through emanations. In the final stage of this emanation of Bindu, it expands to a triangle of iccha shakti, jnana shakti and kriya shakti, according to Christopher Wallis.

When Shiva and Shakti have reached union after the journey back to the source, amrita (nectar of immortality) is poured down the body of the adept. Tara is connected to

57

amrita in her mythology and that might point to a close relationship with Bindu since amrita is said to come from Bindu, according to Swami Satyananda Saraswati.

As the first emanation, Tara is close to absolute truth.

Tara in her journey back to the source is the last step of ego/separate self, merging into the absolute. This dissolution is called pralaya. Since the creation process from Bindu is described as an explosion, maybe her way back to the source can be understood as a form of implosion.

Tara also seems to be connected to Ajna chakra since Para Vac, a tantric goddess who shares Tara's connection to the first sonic vibration of manifestation, is connected to the triangle of powers of iccha, jnana and kriya shakti (explained below).

Para Vac is said to be the voice of intuition; pratibha. She is also connected to iccha shakti and thereby to Shushumna.

The Vedic goddess Saraswati connected to the creative sonic vibration/word OM is connected to the buddhi (intellect) as the power of discrimination, placed in the Ajna system. Also, manas (mind), and ahamkara (lit. I-maker, identity) are associated with the Ajna system.

'The word' (OM) also exists on grosser levels as we will see when we talk about the goddess Matangi.

Ajna chakra is said to be the place where the voice of intuition/knowing (pratibha) can be heard and received. This happens as the faculties of buddhi, manas and ahamkara have been purified.

In the Ajna chakra is placed a triangle representing, the three main energy channels. These energy channels are connected to iccha, jnana and kriya shakti.

Iccha shakti is connected to Shushumna (the central energy channel). Kriya shakti to Ida (left main energy channel). Jnana shakti to Pingala (right main energy channel).

These three channels Shushumna, Ida and Pingala are said to unite in the placement of Ajna

Tripurasundari

Tripurasundari symbolizes the impulse of will (iccha shakti) in its form as desire directed towards the world and as the ability to enjoy the individuated expression of the divine, as manifested.

She also symbolizes the ability to turn that will and longing towards the divine (from the root 'div' in Sanskrit, meaning shining) and towards uniting with the greater will.

In these roles, she symbolizes both the binding and the liberating force of desire.

She is the first in the triad of iccha, jnana and kriya shakti.

This is because iccha (the impulse of desire that leads to will) leads to the structure of how and ends with action being taken, according to the creation process in this tradition.

Tripurasundari is also connected to Bindu as Kameshwari (lady of desire) in union with Shiva as Kameshwara (lord of desire). They are said to be made of red and white light.

Bhuvaneshwari

Bhuvaneshwari is the limitation of 'infinite light' into 'space' that happens as manifestation occurs from 'Prakasha' to 'akasha', according to Kavitha Chinnaiyan.

Bhuvaneshwari might be connected to maya as the dividing principle in tantric tradition, creating multiplicity.

She is the dividing and organizing principle of knowledge (jnana). As such she creates/is the matrix of this world.

She is connected to prakriti (pra-before, kriti-creation), that which is creation and lies beyond creation.

She is what constitutes the physical creation as the elements, also in the form of the individual body.

She is also connected to the indiyas (mental capacities) of the human organism, which are connected to the elements.

Bhairavi

Bhairavi is connected to the action principle as kriya shakti.

Her name comes from the words bharana (to create), ramana (to protect) and vamana (to emit), all words that identify her with the act of creation and upholding of creation.

In her journey back to source, it is said that at the end of the cosmic world cycle, Bhairavi dissolves the world in her form as fire, which also connects her to destruction.

As connected to creation (srsti), preservation (stihiti) and dissolution (samhara), she seems to symbolizes three of the acts of Shiva (the name of God/Light of consciousness in the Shaiva Tantra).

Bhairavi is connected to the heat of life force and the heat generated by directing that force into spiritual practice. She represents the focus and effort needed to reach the spiritual goal of transformation. As such she is sometimes called Tripurabhairavi and represents the rising of Kundalini. In this symbology, she forms a pair with Tripurasundari who is connected to the descending grace in the form of amrita, which follows that work. The couple Tripurasundari and

Tripurabhairavi may also be symbolic of upper and lower Kundalini (see more under 'The Kundalini Process').

Together Tripurasundari, Bhuvaneshwari and Bhairavi might symbolize that you need to offer all your will, all your knowing and all your power of action to reach the divine.

This would fit well with Chinnamasta. Chinnamasta may symbolize the principle of total surrender.

Chinnamasta

Chinnamasta symbolizes both the concealing (tirodhana) of the underlying unity of all that is but also the revelation (anugraha) of that unity. As a concealing power, she creates a feeling of separation and individuality; as a revealing power, she exposes that separation as illusory, according to Kavitha Chinnaiyan.

If Bhairavi was connected to the first three acts of Shiva, Chinnamasta seems connected to the last two; concealment (tirodhana) and revelation (anugraha).

Chinnamasta is connected to the extremely strong and focused force of lightning.

Kundalini is often referred to as lightning-like.

Chinnamasta is connected to sexual energy (desire, Tripurasundari) turned upwards through the central energy channel (Shushumna).

In Chinnamasta's origin myth, Parvati (Shakti) is making love with Shiva in the reverse position with Parvati on top. As Shiva reaches climax, Parvati turns into a fierce form named Prachanda Kali. From her body emerge two shaktis, Dakini and Varnini, who become her attendants. Parvati then goes with her attendants to the river to wash. After some time, the attendants get hungry and ask Parvati for food. When not able to wait until they get home, Chinnamasta severs her head with her fingernails and feeds them and herself with three bloodstreams coming out from her neck. The left bloodstream satisfies Dakini, the right Varnini and the central bloodstream herself as the severed head.

Chinnamasta's attendant Dakini symbolizes kriya shakti (creative force) and her attendant Varnini symbolizes jnana shakti (division, knowledge). Kriya shakti is connected to Ida and jnana shakti is connected to Pingala.

The symbology makes it clear that the source of nourishment for everything is the divine (unseparated) energy said to be able to flow in the Shushumna, represented by Chinnamasta herself.

The symbology also shows the role of sexuality in the energy flow of the body. Because of the vagueness of Shiva climaxing or not (one version of the myth says he didn't), the symbology can be interpreted in two ways.

It can be understood as symbolizing the upturned energy flowing back to the source (withholding the climax) instead of into manifestation. It can also symbolize the manifestation process starting with the appearance of Ida and Pingala in the form of Dakini and Varnini.

This symbology can be understood as the appearance of the powers of iccha (Shushumna), jnana (Ida) and kriya (Pingala) as the first division of the first emanation of creative force as Tara. It can also symbolize the union of these three energy channels in Ajna on the journey back to source/Bindu.

Iccha shakti is the primary desire that underlies the creation of the world and that turns our longing towards the transient world. That desire is the same that turns, after being tired of the transient world, back to the source (see Tripurasundari).

This is the journey into and out of manifestation (more about this in 'The Kundalini Process').

Iccha shakti is connected to Shushumna, the central energy channel also associated with Chinnamasta.

The offering of the head has been an ancient symbol of total surrender in Indian spirituality, both in animal sacrifices (made by decapitation) and in human sacrifice, symbolic or physical.

Another of Chinnamasta's myths says that she severs her head after having received amrita (nectar of immortality) to prevent the demons from taking share in it. Oral yogic tradition often says that when the energy has reached the placement of Vishuddhi chakra in the neck, it will not descend again. This might mean that the amrita flowing down from the top of the head can only be enjoyed after fully offering one's egoistical tendencies, a complete surrender, an offering of the head.

Vishuddhi chakra is also connected to purification, in the tantric tradition meaning returning to unity, 'vi' meaning very and 'shuddi' meaning 'pure'. This return to unity at Vishuddhi is said to go through the letters of the Sanskrit alphabet since the tantric cosmology says that the manifest universe is sonic in its nature.

Another interesting parallel is that in another version of the same myth ('The churning of the ocean of milk'), Shiva is said to drink a poison that arises as they churn the cosmic ocean for amrita and controls it by holding it in his throat. His throat turns blue from the poison and gives him the name Nilakantha (blue throat). Swami Satyananda Saraswati says that the nectar of immortality (amrita) is divided into nectar and poison at Vishuddhi. The religious scholar Lilian Silburn has found in her research that Kundalini is described as poison in her unliberated state and as the nectar of immortality in her liberated state. Here again, we see the theme of desire both as binding and liberating, as bringing both division as well as unity.

The severed head can be seen as representing liberation, an expanded consciousness. There are Buddhist Tantras supporting this interpretation of the severed head as the offering of egoistical tendencies and the result as an expanded awareness.

Chinnmamasta can then be seen as the result of the fully upturned power (because of an upturned desire to return to source/unity) of the individual, piercing the granthis (blockages) along the central energy channel (Sushumna). Several of her names point to this: Shushumnavarabhasini (she who understands the sound of the Shushumna nadi), Sahasraradalamadhyastha (she who is established in the thousand petal lotus (Sahasrara).

The force of Kundalini when these granthis (blockages) along the central channel are pierced, is so forceful that it 'blows the head off'. Here, the individual consciousness gets united with the cosmic consciousness in Sahasrara outside the scull (lower and the upper Kundalini, read more under 'The Kundalini Process').

Dhumavati

Dhumavati means 'the smokey one'.

Dhumavati is connected to pralaya as the end of time. She might also be connected to the end of a cycle represented by the lunar phase of the black moon.

She is connected to the state of deep sleep where consciousness is lost. This can be seen in one of her original myths where Sita swallows Shiva (Light of consciousness/Ground of Being) down. In this myth, it is said that after Sita had swallowed Shiva down, smoke began to come out of her body. That smoke was her illusory power (maya). That smoke became the goddess Dhumavati.

As we can see the Ground of Being/Light of consciousness (Shiva) can never really be lost, only concealed. Dhumavati on her journey into creation might be understood as this illusory concealing power of maya. Dhumavati's connection to smoke might also be a symbol of the element of air as the main carrier of Prana (life force) which is the most subtle manifestation of the non-physical.

Dhumavati's other main myth tells that she was created by the smoke that came from Sati as she burned herself to ashes. This seems to be a symbol of her nature as the disappointments of life (more about this when we talk about the next goddess Bhagalamukhi).

If we can assert that Chinnamasta is connected to the Vishuddhi chakra as one of the placements of the elements along the central channel, here placed at the throat as given by the tantric school of Kubjika, then Dhumavati can be understood as connected to the Anahatha chakra placed at the heart, connected to smoke as a symbol for the element of air and Prana (life force).

Anahata chakra is visualized as two triangles facing up and down respectively, intertwined as the star of Salomon in the Hebrew tradition. It is visualized as having a smokey color symbolizing air.

Anahatha chakra is connected to Prana (life force). Air is said to be the main carrier of Prana, the most subtle manifestation of the non-physical. Prana creates a sound; nada, that has given name to this chakra. Anahatha means unstruck and refers to this unstruck sound.

Manas is connected to the heart since our thoughts and feelings are said to reside here. Since Dhumavati is about meeting the disappointments in life she might symbolize the state of non-attachment to the world that arises through disappointment, which is the prerequisite for the surrender that follows on the upward journey with Chinnamasta.

Dhumavati as the smoke of the ashes of Sita as proposed by the myth, as air and as Prana; a subtle form of manifestation, as transformed grosser materiality (by the fire) can then be seen as symbolizing non-attachment to the gross, transient, divided (illusory) experience of the world.

Bhagalamukhi

Bhagalamukhi is connected to stopping and stilling.

In one of her origin myths, she is brought forth from the goddess Tripurasundari (described above) as the god Vishnu does austerities by a sacred pond to stop a storm threatening to destroy the world. The pond where Bhagalamukhi appeared, named turmeric, might be the reason for her association with the color yellow, but it might also be connected to Vishnu who is associated with the color yellow. However in this myth, the color yellow seems connected to the power of stopping or stilling.

Bhagalamukhi is said to be the giver of Vac Siddhi; the power of manifestation by speech (compare with Kalpa Vriksha) and to be the one who takes it away. In one of her myths, she stops a demon who has gotten Vac Siddhi by grasping his tongue. In this form, Bhagalamukhi can be understood as the one who stops the misuse of the power of manifestation, represented by Matangi in her form as being bound to the transient world and by the desire for power (see more below).

The yogic practice of breath retention (kumbhaka) can be seen as associated with Bhagalamukhi as a practice of stopping or holding. It is also a practice of internalizing the energy.

Bhagalamukhi is said to be the first in the army of Tripurasundari. Tripurasundari is connected to iccha shakti and therefore to Shushumna. Bhagalamukhi being the first in the army of Tripurasundari might symbolize that Bhagalamukhi as kumbhaka is the coming together of the five breaths (the five pranas/energies of the body) in the kanda/navel area and the rising of Kundalini through Shushumna. More about this in the coming chapter!

In another of her origin myths (referred to above), Bhagalamukhi is said to have been created when Sita swallowed Shiva. The smoke (maya) became Dhumavati. The goddess swallowing Shiva became known as Bhagalamukhi, as she swallowed him whole like a crane. Bhagalamukhi means 'she who has the head/face of a crane'. Shiva cursed her as well as Dhumavati to be widows (without him).

Bhagalamukhi as a state without contact with, and separated from, the Ground of being/Light of consciousness

(Shiva) is said to lead us to be drawn in and paralyzed by the world; the manifest.

As such, she might be understood as the projection of the Light of consciousness into a world. Her possible connection to Prana fits well with this since Prana is the most subtle manifestation of the non-physical. This might be why her shadow side is the ability to paralyze motion, initiative and thought, all regulated by Prana. Bhagalamukhi might be connected to the Kalpa Vriksha; a wish-fulfilling tree said to reside below Anahatha chakra. This can be understood as the power that comes from centering energy into the force of Kundalini that is said to happen in Manipura chakra.

If the connection to kumbhaka is correct, Bhagalamukhi may be associated with Manipura chakra and the navel area (kanda) where the breath is held and all the pranas of the body are held together in kumbhaka (breath pause). The pranas of the in-breath and the out-breath are said to be the sun and the moon. Manipura is said to shine from the light of the sun and moon as jewels (mani-jewel, pura-city/place) which also might explain the color of Bhagalamukhi.

If we look at this idea, then the myth when Sita burns herself up in (or at the place of) the sacrificial fire might take on a related meaning.

In this myth, Sita (Shakti) and Shiva are the only ones not invited to the fire sacrifice of Daksha, Sita's father. This fire ritual was meant to establish the sacrificial ritual and all the gods' roles in it. The fire ritual in India is as old as the oldest Vedas and its practice was the most important spiritual practice in India, as in many other places of the world.

In this myth, the minor god Daksha doesn't invite Shiva or Shakti, the highest of the gods/goddesses in the Shaivaite tradition, to this most important spiritual ritual. In one version of the myth, Daksha says that the reason for not inviting Shiva is that he lacks lineage and consorts with unclean beings (reminiscent of what Christ also was told). This upsets Sita (Shakti) so much that in one version of the myth, she burns herself up with her inner heat; tapas. Tapas in the tantric tradition was linked to the heat of the life force (Prana).

Before the advent of the tantric tradition, the religious practices in India had become more and more internalized over many hundreds of years, but the practice of the outer fire ritual conducted by the priests/brahmins was still very prevalent. This myth might be understood as an internalization of the Vedic fire ritual in tantric tradition.

Bhagalamukhi could as such be understood as the fire (Kundalini) generated in the navelarea, by holding breath retention (kumbakha) of the breaths (pranas) of the moon and sun together with the rest of the pranas of the body. As the force of Kundalini, she would in this case be connected to Shushumna which we have seen that she is.

Matangi

Matangi is sometimes described as the tantric form of Saraswati. She is often depicted with a Veena as is Saraswati. She is connected to the creative process just like Saraswati.

Matangi is connected to the spoken word, 'vaikari vac'. This is the creative word that started with Tara at its most supreme level; OM. This level of the word binds us to the transient world or becomes an expression of the supreme word into manifestation.

One of Matangi's myths points to this. In this myth, she is born from the leftovers, 'the ucchista' of the highest gods and

69

goddesses. The higher gods and goddesses of this myth might represent the supreme word and 'the ucchista' might represent the 'vaikari vac'; the word as an expression of erotic/creative impulse into manifestation.

Her name means 'she whose limbs are intoxicated' (with passion).

Her connection to the word is also closely related to creativity and one of her colors, emerald green, is connected to the creative force and fertility of nature.

David Kinsley believes a precursor of Matangi exists in a Buddhist text in the form of a girl named Prakriti (nature). In this text, Prakriti tries to, together with her mother, lure the closest disciple of Buddha into marriage. This seems to be the theme of the temptations of the transient world.

In one of Matangi's myths, Shiva becomes a low-caste man as he makes love with Parvati (Shakti) a low-caste woman. This together with Matangis association with 'vaikari vac' points to that Matangi is the 'the lowest' form of creative expression of the divine into the physical (gross) universe.

Matangi's symbology fits well with Svadhistana chakra as the center of lust. Svadhistana is also connected to water; the element of fertility and creativity which are other associations of Matangi.

Her binding face is connected to the attachment to power as some myths describe her as the goddess to evoke power over others, as well as the power of attraction and of attaining one's desires.

Bagalamukhi as the projection of the Light of consciousness into a world as Prana might point to Matangi being the feeling of needing to fill oneself up, as lacking something and therefore craving the power to get something from outside oneself. This appears after entering an experience of separation, in the tantric tradition called anavamala. This fits well with the Svadhistana chakra´s connection to desire as a binding force binding us to transient life (samsara).

Her liberating side seems to be the ability to transcend the desire/will for power. One of her myths points to this, as it places Matangi as someone who is required to be worshipped before Shiva, turning the tables on the Brahminical order of higher and lower.

Matangi is connected to the conch shell and so is Kundalini in her coiled form. As Kundalini is said to be the coil produced by withdrawing all of the energies of the body (pancha vayus) to the navel area where Svadhistana chakra is located, Matangi on her way to liberation might be this coil.

In her liberated state, she is the spontaneous action; kriya, and the authentic voice. As the authentic voice, she is an expression of the supreme word and the voice of intuition; pratibha.

Kamala

Kamala means 'she of the lotus'. In her association with the lotus, she represents the transcendence of the limitations of the world as well as the life force (Prana) that pervades all of creation.

She is connected to the Vedic goddesses Sri and Lakshmi. Sri means auspicious.

Kamala is depicted as being bathed with nectar by two or four large elephants.

Elephants are in Indian tradition associated with clouds and rain and therefore with fertility. Elephants are also associated with authority.

Since the elephants pouring nectar over Kamala are sometimes said to be four, she might be connected to the element earth and therefore to the Muladhara chakra. The element earth in Muladhara chakra is symbolized by an elephant with four trunks, representing stability. Kamala is like Matangi associated with prakriti (nature). Here probably as the principle of making manifest.

Kamala is being bathed by nectar and one of Lakshmi's earliest associations is with the god Soma, meaning nectar. Soma is the sap of life (life force) but is also associated with the deathless nectar (amrita) residing in the Sahasrara and said to be drawn down into the body of the adept after union with God/Light of consciousness, has taken place making the body immortal (see more under 'The Kundalini Process').

In the Kankalamalini Tantra, it is said that Shakti after her union with Shiva returns from Sahasrara to Muladhara. With her, she is said to bring the amrita stored in the Sahasrara, which is said to make the person an expression of Shiva/ Light of consciousness.

Lakshmi's central myth 'The churning of the ocean of milk' also associates or identifies her with the nectar of immortality (amrita).

The word 'kamala' is used to refer to the union of Shiva and Shakti; as the light radiance of their union.

Lakshmi is connected to the radiance of golden yellow and rosy red.

Amrita is said to accompany Kundalini (Shakti) down to Muladhara.

As amrita Kamala is also associated with a chakra said to exist inside Anahatha chakra; Hrit chakra, a chakra said to be visualised inside the physical heart. A nadi (amrita nadi) from the Sahasrara is said to channel the nectar of immortality (amrita) to this place, according to Sally Kempton.

In oral tradition, it is sometimes said that after the union of Shiva and Shakti in the Sahasrara, and the descent of amrita saturating the body, making it immortal, Shiva and Shakti rest united in the heart area; Anahatha. This is also found in the symbology of Anahatha as two triangles, one with the tip turned up representing Shiva and one with the tip turned down representing Shakti, interlaced as a star.

Swami Satyanda Saraswati states that it is at the level of the heart that descending grace (amrita) is made manifest to the world. This manifestation of descending grace might be understood as satyam (truth), shivam (goodness) and sundaram (beauty). These are the highest forms of iccha, kriya and jnana shakti.

The Vedic form of Kamala, Lakshmi is connected to Vishnu. Vishnu is connected to the law of righteousness.

Before Lakshmi became the consort of Vishnu, she was said to be fickle. This points to the two faces of Lakshmi. One symbolizes the attachment to the manifest universe, following whatever gives the most pleasure, and the other symbolizes faithfulness to the law of righteousness, serving that law in the world.

Kamala is given as the last of the Mahavidyas. David Kinsley points out that this might mean that Kamala is the least important or the most important of the Mahavidyas; as a starting point or a result. In the layout I have given here, Kamala is both. She is the starting point as the attachment to and trying to find fulfilment through the manifest, transient world. But in her liberated state, she is also the transcendence of that world, expressing itself in the world, reforming it.

As the lotus, she unites earth, water, air, and transcendence (the flower) by having her roots in the earth, with her stalk moving through water and air. The stalk here might be understood as the Shushumna (the central channel). The lotus flower on the top may be understood as the Sahasrara; the thousand-petaled lotus (see more under 'The Kundalini Process').

In some of her name hymns, she is identified with several of the other Mahavidyas; Tara, Matangi, Dhumavati; Kali and Bhairavi. This might reinforce the notion that she is the starting point and the result of the Kundalini process, an expression of all the faces of the Goddess (Shakti).

Death and Resurrection

According to David Kinsley, the Mahavidyas form a process of death and resurrection often seen in shamanic and mystic tradition, an experience of death and being rebuilt as spiritual beings with spiritual powers that go beyond the gross, transient world.

The Kundalini Process

Samavesha, Shaktipat, Anugraha, Urdhva Kundalini, Adha Kundalini

According to Christopher Wallis, Rudra shakti samavesha refers to an immersion into divine (from the root 'div' meaning shining) power (shakti).

Shaktipata means the descent of divine power. In the dualist Shaiva Tantra, shaktipata was a sign of a calling from Shiva. Shaktipata refers to a stronger infusion of power than samavesha usually refers to and happens only once or twice in a person's life, according to Wallis in his book *Tantra Illuminated.*

The strongest form of shaktipata kills the body and ends the cycle of rebirth.

The second strongest form of shaktipata gives intuitive insight leading to full liberation. Sometimes the intuition needs to be strengthened by a guru and/or scripture. After this has happened, the divine power is always present in that person.

There are also lesser degrees of shaktipata.

Shaktipata as a descent of divine power might be referring to what is sometimes called the descent of upper Kundalini.

Anugraha means that which follows grasping, maybe referring to attachment (see Bhagalamukhi) and may be seen as a return to the unity with God/Light of consciousness from a state of contraction and separation. It means revealing, remembrance and revelation and is said to happen as we are getting tired of the transient world and are called back/or long to go back to the source.

Anugraha might be connected to what is called lower Kundalini.

Christopher Wallis highlights a verse often given in Kaula tantric texts with unknown origin.

Translation by Christopher Wallis.

The one who has experienced immersion into Rudra shakti (God's power) due to the descent of the upper power, and the contraction of the lower power, that person is a truly wise one (has insight into the nature of reality).

According to Christopher Wallis, Ksemaraja in the tantric text, Pratnabijahridayam talks about this verse as referring to what he calls upper (urdhva) and lower (adha) Kundalini.

The union of upper and lower Kundalini seems to result in the union of the individual with God/Light of consciousness.

The yogi and philosopher Sri Aurobindo says in his book The Mother:

There are two powers that alone can effect in their conjunction the great and difficult thing which is the aim of

76

*our endeavour, a fixed and unfailing aspiration that calls
from below and a supreme Grace from above that answers.*

Understanding the process of the Mahavidyas and how the
process is here described in this verse, it might even be the
other way around. Divine power calls us and waits for us to
answer the call.

Kundalini Related Experiences in Other Cultural Contexts

Swami Satyananda Saraswati points out in his book *Kundalini Tantra* that experiences similar to Kundalini have been recorded in other cultural contexts.

One of the examples that he brings up is the n/um phenomenon of the !Kung people of Botswana. The n/um is described as hot and as lifting you in your belly and in your back, and making you shiver. It is described as taking you into the !kia state where a different form of vision occurs. It also brings with it a healing power.

Another example given is the Daoist tradition where the chi, the vital force/life force, after it has been accumulated in the lower belly, is said to burst out and begin to flow in energy channels in the body causing pain, warmth, coldness, internal lights and sounds and a feeling of inner movement, among other things. It is also said to sometimes result in the physical body radiating light.

There are interesting similarities to this description in the transfiguration of Christ and of Moses radiating face after speaking to God, as we have seen. The same phenomenon might be described in this passage about John the Baptist:

John 5:35

John was a lamp that burned and gave light, and you chose for a time to enjoy his light.

Lastly, Satyanda brings up the medieval saint Theresa of Avila. In the passage he has chosen, she describes noises in her head resembling brimming rivers and birds whistling at the top of her head. Satyananda compares this to the nada phenomenon of the Kundalini experience which in the process of ascension is said to cause a sound as one has reached the level of the heart, Anahatha chakra and then different sounds as it rises up through the head to the top of the head, birds whistling being one, the sound of waters another. Sounds of thunder and burning wood at the top of the head are also described in the tantric tradition.

Theresa understands the sounds as being the spirit moving upwards and understands the upper part of the head as the part where the soul is said to be.

The Chakra System

The chakras/lotuses are to be visualized in places along the central channel where we have stuck karmic energy. This stuck karmic energy blocks the Shushumna and therefore access to Sahasrara and the store of amrita here.

The amrita as it is drawn into the body totally heals and replenishes it. This nectar is said to impart the yogi with the highest spiritual knowing, the body with deathlessness and the person becomes an expression of Shiva/God/Light of consciousness.

Professor and expert on Hatha Yoga, James Mallison, explains the chakras of Tantra as visualizations connected to the elements, grosser elements the further down they are. By meditation on them, it was thought one could reverse the creation process back to the Bindu where the first emanation happened.

The energy of the individual is here referred to as Shakti and the source as Shiva.

One can place the chakras in different ways along the central channel and there can be less or more chakras according to the tantric tradition. This is one example that originated from the Kubjika School of Tantra.

The visualizations of the energy system may be done in different ways but they are said to have been developed from experiences of tantric masters.

Shushumna

Shushumna is the central energy channel of the body. Shusumna is visualized as extending from the pelvic floor to the crown of the head as a column of golden or cobalt blue light with a width of an arrow shaft, according to Christopher Wallis.

Shushumna is also referred to as 'madhya nadi' in the Vijnana Bhairava Tantra. The word madhya means middle. Nadi means channel.

Swami Satyananda Saraswati says that the descent of amrita happens through the Shushumna.

Muladhara

Muladhara is connected to the elements of earth, stability and manifestation. It is connected to sexuality and desires turned towards the manifest world as well as survival.

It is placed in the area of the perineum.

Svadhistana

Svadhistana is connected to the element water, sexuality, creativity, healing, the experience of sweetness in life (rasa), ojas (stored nourishment in the body) deep emotional patterns (samskaras) and instincts. It is also connected to subconscious karmas.

It is connected to the desire that keeps us bound to the cycle of life and rebirth (samsara). It is said that Svadhistana dissolves jealousy in its waters as it awakens. It is placed slightly below the navel in the area of the womb.

Manipura

Manipura is connected to the element fire, personal will and action and the force of transformation in the form of the sacrificial fire; agni.

Manipura is placed in the navel area. Here is also the placement of the Prana called samana in the human body. Samana is an equalizing power that draws the other energies together and takes them back in the form of Kundalini to an undivided state.

It is said that the moon/creative energy (Ida) secretes nectar down to Manipura chakra that is consumed by the sun/action in the material world (Pingala). This leads to old age and death. This can be understood as the process of division leading to creation, called maya. Creation is transient in its nature and must at some point dissolve, leading to old age and death.

Anahatha

Anahatha is connected to the element of vayu (air/wind) and is placed in the heart area.

Rudrayamala Tantra says that vayu in the heart is supreme Brahman without form and sound (nada) with form and that he is life itself (life force/Prana).

The Anahatha area is also the midpoint between the transcendent and the immanent.

In the area of Anahatha chakra, there is said to exist a wish-fulfilling tree; Kalpa Vriksha. When this is activated, it is said that we begin to be able to manifest our thoughts.

One story says that Kalpa vriksha was placed on earth and was transported to the heaven of Indra after people had misused it with evil wishes. It is interesting to note how similar this is to the idea of the Tree of Life (giving eternal life) in the Garden of Eden, that Adam and Eve are prevented from eating from, after having eaten from the Tree of Knowledge and having realised the difference between good and evil and having received the status of gods. Comparing this with the story about the wish-fulfilling tree one may understand this status as gods as the ability to create.

The placement of Kalpa Vriksha in the heart area might be understood as the place where this power no longer will be misused by evil wishes. Anahatha as it is activated is said to turn us from egotism to love.

Another chakra is sometimes visualized in the heart area called Hrit chakra. This chakra is visualized in the physical heart. The nectar of immortality (amrita) is said to be channeled to this place from Sahasrara, after the union between the individual and God/Light of consciousness has taken place, according to Sally Kempton, a close student of Muktananda.

In oral tradition, it is sometimes said that after the union of Shiva and Shakti in the Sahasrara, and the descent of amrita saturating the body, making it immortal, Shiva and Shakti rest united in the heart, maybe as a midpoint between transcendence and immanence. The symbol of the cross of

Salomon in the Anahatha chakra is said to symbolize this union as an upward triangle (Shiva) and a downward triangle (Shakti).

Swami Satyanda Saraswati stated that it is at the level of Anahatha that descending grace (amrita) is made manifest to the world.

Vishuddhi

Vishuddhi is connected to the element of space and is placed in the centre of the throat.

The 16 petals of the Visuddhi are connected to the 16th phase of the full moon, symbolizing completion.

This is the first chakra from the bottom and up that doesn't have any qualities on the petals, the others have mixed positive and negative qualities. On the petals are instead the Sanskrit vowels. These are said to contain both the poison that Shiva holds in his throat and the nectar that drips from the higher centres. Visuddhi's possible connection to Shiva as Nilakantha; bluethroated Shiva, connects Visuddhi to the color blue.

Swami Satyananda Saraswati says that the nectar of immortality (amrita) is divided into nectar and poison at Vishuddhi.

Vishuddhi is also connected to purification, in the tantric tradition meaning returning to unity, 'vi' meaning very and 'shuddhi' meaning 'pure'. This return to unity at Vishuddhi is said to go through the letters of the Sanskrit alphabet since the tantric cosmology says that the manifest universe is sonic in its nature.

Maybe this points to the theme of desire both as binding and liberating, as bringing both division (maya) as well as unity.

Sally Kempton says that Visuddhi is a place of surrender to the higher will. This may point to being a part of a unity.

Ajna

Ajna is found in the center of the head. This is the place of the crossing of the three main nadis (Shushumna, Ida, Pingala) and, says Sally Kempton, of two cranial nerves from the eyes and one up to the crown of the head.

Ajna is sometimes referred to as the third eye or the Spiritual Eye.

Ajna is said to be the place where the voice of intuition (pratibha) can be heard and received. This happens as the faculties of buddhi (intellect), manas (mind) and ahamkara (identity) have been purified.

There is said to be a subtle white flame present in Ajna, called Itara linga. When Ajna is activated, it is said that one becomes a rishi; a seer. It is also said that you start to understand the laws of karma that lead to different effects.

Ajna means 'command'. It is said that the Bindu explodes at the goddess (Shakti) command generating the world through emanations, according to Christopher Wallis. This is according to the Tantric Schools of Kaubjika and Srividya/Traipura.

As Bindu explodes, a triangle with three points of iccha, jnana and kriya shakti is formed. These are associated with the three main nadis (energy channels); Shushumna, Pingala and Ida.

Iccha shakti is connected to Shushumna (the central energy channel). Kriya shakti to Ida (left main energy channel). Jnana shakti to Pingala (right main energy channel).

These three channels; Ida, Pingala and Shushumna are said to unite as Kundalini rises, in the placement of Ajna.

Swami Yogananda called the blue energy found in Ajna 'Christ Consciousness'.

It is interesting to note the lapis lazuli-colored light in the vision of Ezekiel (see Prakasha/Or Ein Sof/kingdom of heaven), the opal blue of Yogananda and the cobalt blue of the tantric visualization of Shushumna.

Swami Yogananda said that there resides a Spiritual Eye in the location of Ajna. The Spiritual Eye has an outer ring of gold, a center of opal blue, and a silver star in the middle.

He understood the golden energy to be the vibration/creation of God and the blue light as the energy of God in creation.

Compare this with the golden and cobalt blue visualization of Shushumna.

The silver star (compare with the mirror-like wisdom quality and Tara) Yogananda understood as God's presence as an extremely concentrated point of energy (see Bindu and Sahasrara).

Sahasrara

Sahasrara is usually not considered to be a chakra since it lies beyond the reach of the energy channels (nadis) of the body. It is also cosmic (all-encompassing) in its nature.

It exists in a void region sometimes said to be filled with water, for example in Rudrayamala Tantra. Ancient Indian tradition states that the creation came out of an infinite body of primordial water (compare with the creation myth in the Old Testament). The void as we have seen in the tantric school of Pratyabhijna is an ocean of light or potential energy pulsating.

The petals of the lotus of the Sahasrara are usually said to consist of all the colors or to be white (the color white consists of all the colors).

Shiva in Sahasrara is sometimes in the Tantras visualized as being of the color of pure crystal.

The tantric text Satchakranirupana says that Sahasrara has a full moon inside, radiating white light. This light is sometimes explained to be the radiation of Bindu. Inside the moon is a lightening-like triangle and inside the triangle is Bindu. Bindu is the union of Shiva and Shakti in their embodied forms.

Bindu is a point of highly concentrated energy from where creation flows and returns. Here, the ray of the individual emanates from or unites with God/Light of consciousness.

In Phetkarini Tantra, it is said that the divine Kundalini arising from Muladhara chakra passes through Shusumna to Vishuddhi chakra and absorbs all creative principles on the way. Kundalini then comes to her own abode in Sahasrara. This is a process of dissolution.

In the Kankalamalini Tantra, it is said that Shakti after her union with Shiva returns from Sahasrara to Muladhara. With her, she is said to bring the amrita stored in the Sahasrara, which is said to make the person an expression of Shiva/ Light of consciousness.

Three bindus, three granthis, three bandhas

In the tantric tradition, three bindus are referred to. A bindu in the sacrum/kanda which represents individuality and embodiment and is red in color. A bindu at the heart which represents the subtle body and is cobalt blue in color. A bindu at the Ajna which is white in color and represents consciousness. These are the main energy centers.

There are said in the Hatha Yoga tradition to be knots; granthis, where especially difficult karmic energy is stored. These are called the knot of Brahma, the knot of Vishnu and the knot of Rudra.

The knot of Brahma located in the sacrum represents attachment to the gross experience of the world and the mode of survival. The knot of Vishnu at the heart represents the emotional attachment to the world as a separate existence. The knot of Rudra at the placement of the Ajna represents attachment to limited knowledge through the means of manas (mind), buddhi (intellect) and ahamkara (identity), a knowledge filtered through the limitation of the separated I.

To be able to 'pierce' these granthis (knots), three energetic bandhas (locks) were used. These are Muladhara bandha, Uddhiyana bandha and Jaladhara bandha. These locks are applied at the sacrum, the navel and the throat. These are applied together for maximum results together with pranayama in Maha bandha and in Maha mudra.

Shushumna and the Stairway to Heaven

An interesting comparison is between the Shushumna (central energy channel) and the symbology of the stairway of Jacob in the Bible, as a vertical movement of divine energies/angels moving up and down, in the case of Christ, in him.

Genesis 28:10–13

Jacob left Beersheba and set out for Harran. When he reached a certain place, he stopped for the night because the sun had set. Taking one of the stones there, he put it under his head and lay down to sleep. He had a dream in which he saw a stairway resting on the earth, with its top reaching to heaven, and the angels of God were ascending and descending on it. There above it stood the LORD, and he said, "I am the LORD, the God of your Father Abraham and the God of Isaac…

Jesus speaks of angels ascending and descending on the Son of Man. Here 'Son of Man' probably refers to himself.

John 1:47–51

When Jesus saw Nathanael approaching, he said of him, "Here truly is an Israelite in whom there is no deceit."

"How do you know me?" Nathanael asked.

Jesus answered, "I saw you while you were still under the fig tree before Philip called you."

Then Nathanael declared, "Rabbi, you are the Son of God; you are the king of Israel."

Jesus said, "You believe because I told you I saw you under the fig tree. You will see greater things than that." He then added, "Very truly I tell you, you will see 'heaven open, and the angels of God ascending and descending on the Son of Man'."

Kundalini Yoga

The process of uniting upper and lower Kundalini is later given the name Kundalini Yoga in the Tantras.

This was a pan-tantric practice done by all the schools of Tantra, according to Christopher Tompkins religious scholar specializing in Tantra and Sanskritist. Here Kundalini Yoga does not refer to the Kundalini Yoga of Yogi Bhajan, but is the traditional name of a tantric practice. Kundalini Yoga means the application of Kundalini, according to Christopher Tompkins.

Tompkins describes the practice as such. The practice was to visualize Shiva's primal shakti at the third eye in the shape of a coil emerging from a seed point (bindu). This was then drawn down to the navel through the lunar in-breath. Here it was held in breath retention (kumbakha) together with the withheld solar out-breath and the rest of the five vital breaths/pranas/energies of the body (pancha vayus). All the energies were drawn to the navel area where they created a coil of Shiva's power, which was then raised up through the central channel adding mantra and visualization with the exhalation.

Tompkins explains that the coil of energy created by breath pause at the third eye and the navel was what was referred to as Kundalini. He refers to the tantric master Brahmananda who defines Kundalini as the shakti held still (sthitaha). Brahmananda says that Kundalini is the power of creation, according to Christopher Tompkins.

According to the translation of Tompkins, Rudrayamala Tantra says that Kundalini is that moment in the breath when shakti coils (breath pause). It also says that when shakti becomes coiled, this is the shape of pure consciousness that begins to pulsate. Kundalini is defined as a vibrational vortex that is formed by the five pranas (pancha vayus) drawn into one point. Samana vayu draws them together in the navel area.

The concentrated energy of Kundalini was often described as lightning-like.

Kundalini was also likened to fire and was often visualised as fire up to the Anahatha area, as sun up to the Ajna area and as moon up to Sahasrara where she became turya (beyond).

According to Christopher Wallis, the energetic in-breath is called the moon and the energetic out-breath is called the sun in many tantric scriptures. They are symbolized by the colors white and red and are then referred to as white bindu and red bindu. Together, in fusion, they are said to create fire (a different state of more concentrated energy/Prana) in the form of Kundalini which moves up Shushumna (the central channel) along the spine.

The normal energetic breath was said to enter the left energy channel Ida and leave through the right energy channel Pingala. To make these breaths fuse into the more concentrated energy of Kundalini and rise up the central channel, the in (apana) and out (prana) breaths were extended, Mulha bandha was applied together with kumbhaka (breath pause) in the navel area to draw the other pranas of the body (vayus) together with the in and out breaths (apana, prana) to make them enter the central channel: Shushumna. Application of a Kundalini mantra as well as visualization was made.

According to Wallis, this practice presumes that the person has received shaktipat and thereby has been infused with God's power and therefore has an enlivened energy system.

The fused energies/breaths/vayus in the form of a coil (Kundalini) in the navel area becomes a fire (concentrated energy) that rises up the central channel to cleanse all karmic impurity.

Tompkins explains that the chakras (energy centers) are purified of all the karmas, by being immersed into amrita in Sahasrara. Then Kundalini is visualized as being regenerated at Ajna as a coil and the chakras are reinstalled at their locations again, from Vishuddhi to Muladhara. The body is stated to obtain a deathless state by this process. The nectar is also said to impart the yogi with the highest spiritual knowing and the person becomes an expression of Shiva/Light of consciousness.

Karma and Sin

It is easy to see the similarities between the description of Kundalini Yoga and the baptism with Holy Spirit and fire in the teaching of Christ. They are described as cleansing from sin or from karma. Both are described as fire. Both are described as the divine; Spirit or Shiva/Shakti.

The karmas are the result of the natural law by which actions determine future modes of a person's existence. These karmas are what is purified in the process of Kundalini Yoga.

It is not difficult to see the similarities with sin as wrong action which results in sickness and death. Christ talks about sickness on many occasions as the result of sin.

Some of the things that the disciples of Christ healed were handicaps that people were born with (Acts 3:1–10).

This can be understood as the result of original sin, but if this interpretation of what Christ taught is not accepted, it might also point to the result of previous actions in other lives.

Christ refers to John the Baptist as Elijah. This might point to the idea of reincarnation.

Matthew 17:10–13

The disciples asked him, "Why then do the teachers of the law say that Elijah must come first?"

Jesus replied, "To be sure, Elijah comes and will restore all things. But I tell you, Elijah has already come, and they did not recognize him, but have done to him everything they wished. In the same way, the Son of Man is going to suffer at their hands." Then the disciples understood that he was talking to them about John the Baptist.

Even if we don't accept this verse as proof of reincarnation in Christ's teaching, Christ uses sin in this life as an explanation for sickness and death.

He also heals by the forgiveness of sins.

There are several examples in the Bible where Christ teaches that even a multitude of sins can be forgiven as long as one repents.

In non-dual Shaiva Tantra, it was believed that karma only had to be lived through as long as one needed it to return to unity with God/Light of consciousness. It seems from these traditions that our lives are constantly created out of the consequences of our actions. We are constantly creating our lives by our actions.

It also seems as if repentance/turning away from our old ways can alter our lives. Our debts can be written off.

Maybe the notion of Kalpa Vriksha (the wish-fulfilling tree) in Tantra points to the realization of our constant influence on our lives, and the possibility of consciously creating our lives within the constraints of what the higher law of consequence allows.

The consequence can be understood to be part of the truth as its results point back to the underlying truth, giving us a lesson or a deeper understanding.

It's interesting to compare the story of Kalpa Vriksha (wish-fulfilling tree) with the fall from Eden. In both of these stories, the Kalpa Vriksha and the Tree of Life (giving eternal life) are made inaccessible to human kind.

In non-dual Shaiva Tantra, it is said that when the individual is formed, it maintains the creative functions of the greater all but in a limited form. It is believed that only when the individual unites with the larger unity, the creative functions become unlimited again.

There is another mythological parallel in the ancient Indian story of 'The churning of the ocean of milk' where the dark forces (asuras) are not allowed to take a part of the nectar of immortality; amrita.

These stories might point to that as long as our wishes are not in alignment with truth and life, all we will manifest will be untruth and death. The temptations of Buddha and Christ may be understood as the temptation to use the power of creation to create what is untrue, transient, separate and that must lead to death.

Good and Evil

Truth and Falsehood, Order and Chaos

Most scholars agree that the founder of Zoroastrianism; Zarathustra lived somewhere in the first millennium BCE.

Zoroastrianism is both monotheistic and has a dualistic cosmology of good and evil. It is believed to have influenced the Abrahamic religions with beliefs such as monotheism, including a dualistic cosmology of good and evil, heaven and hell, good forces and evil forces, judgement after death and a final defeat of evil by a messianic figure, a Saoshyant by a last judgement. This last judgement and the possibility to choose good or evil was due to the free will of humans.

It is believed that two groups of people related culturally and linguistically migrated from the steppes down into the Middle East and Iran respectively into the northwestern part of India, in the second half of the second millennium BCE. It is believed that this is the reason behind the many similarities between early Iranian and Indian religions.

The central part of both religions described in the Vedas and the Avesta (the first book of Zoroastrianism) is a sacrificial offering (Avestan yasna, Vedic yajna) and the usage of an intoxicating liquid (Avestan haoma, Vedic soma). The leader of the sacrifice was the Avestan zautar/Vedic hotar. The ritual was meant to uphold cosmic and ethical order in Avestan called asha, in Vedic tradition called rita. This order was connected in Zoroastrianism to the main deity called Ahura Mazda, the creator and only true existence (the wise lord). The evil forces were those of disorder and chaos. Order (asha) was connected to truth and chaos was connected to falsehood (drug/druj). Asha was also connected to the life force. Living according to goodness and truth was central to Zoroastrianism.

Rita of the Vedas was also connected to truth and the life force.

Dharma is the term used for what upholds rita such as righteousness.

There is also a common usage for terms related to good and evil forces called asuras/ahuras and daivas/daevas in Avestan respectively Vedic language (Sanskrit). Their respective meanings have though become reversed so that the names of the evil forces in the Vedas have become the name of the good forces in Avesta and vice versa. Also, some of the good forces in the Vedas are in the Avesta considered evil forces, such as Indra.

The earliest books of the Vedas, the *Rig Veda*, are believed to have been written somewhere around 1500-1000 BCE.

The evil forces of chaos and falsehood (drug/druj) in Zoroastrianism have their counterpart in the term maya as falsehood or illusion in Vedic tradition.

The school of Advaita Vedanta explains maya as wrong perception and understanding of the world. The belief is that there is an absolute truth behind the ordinary perception of the world. In non-dual Tantra, maya is the diversified experience of the world in contrast to the unified experience of the world.

Druj/drug is explained as uncreated, non-existent and as an antithesis of existence. This fits well with the Advaita Vedantic understanding of maya.

The concept of falsehood and illusion as well as the non-existence of it, can also be found in the Gospel of Truth. Here it is described as without root and as inherently weak since it lacks existential ground.

Gospel of Truth, translation by Robert M. Grant.

For this reason, do not take error too seriously. Thus, since it had no root, it was in a fog as regards the Father, engaged in preparing works and forgetfulnesses and fears in order, by these means, to beguile those of the middle and to make them captive.

Gospel of Truth states that error 'was' because of the forgetfulness of the Father of truth. As we have seen Christ talks about himself as a witness of truth and as someone who gives knowledge of the Father/God.

Gospel of Truth, translation by Robert M. Grant.

This ignorance of the Father brought about terror and fear. And terror became dense like a fog, that no one was able to see. Because of this, error became strong. But it worked on its hylic substance vainly, because it did not know the truth. It was in a fashioned form while it was preparing, in power and in beauty, the equivalent of truth. This then, was not a humiliation for him, that illimitable, inconceivable one. For they were as nothing, this terror and this forgetfulness and this figure of falsehood, whereas this established truth is unchanging, unperturbed and completely beautiful.

Interestingly enough, the equivalent of the tantric idea of maya as diversity in contrast to unity can also be found here.

Gospel of Truth, translation by Robert M. Grant.

By means of unity each one will understand itself. By means of knowledge it will purify itself of diversity with a view towards unity, devouring matter within itself like fire and darkness by light, death by life.

Challenge for the Sake of Good or Yokeless

Satan (Greek diabolos, English devil) means opponent or adversary. The word satan is used in the Old Testament as someone blocking or challenging someone else. This blocking can be as protection, temptation or as a challenge.

In the fourth Book of Moses, the angel of God identifies itself as satan as it stops Bileam from choosing a path that will lead him to destruction.

In the temptation of Christ, the devil is presented as a tempter.

In the *Book of Job*, Satan is the title of an angel under God's command being allowed to test the righteousness of Job.

Belial used for what is wicked in the Old Testament means lacking worth or yokeless. It is interesting to note the similarity with the term yoga in the Vedas meaning to be yoked, later in the Vedas referring to being yoked to God. We will soon see the same theme in the symbology of the goat in the New Testament as not being under God's reign.

The name Beelzebub in the Bible referred to the Canaan god Baal (Hadad). Baal was a god of fertility and natural forces. One of the practices used in the worship of Baal was sacrificing children. Since the Jews considered worship of Baal to be idolatry and maybe also because of its connection to shameful practices that became forbidden in the Judaic tradition, this name developed with time into a name for evil forces.

In Leviticus 20, a prohibition against sacrificing one's children to pagan gods is mentioned.

2 Kings 16:2-4

Ahaz was twenty years old when he became king, and he reigned in Jerusalem sixteen years. Unlike David his father, he did not do what was right in the eyes of the LORD his God. He followed the ways of the kings of Israel and even sacrificed his son in the fire, engaging in the detestable practices of the nations the LORD had driven out before the Israelites. He offered sacrifices and burned incense at the high places, on the hilltops and under every spreading tree.

The goat was in the Old Testament sometimes used as a symbol for the bearer of sin as the scapegoat/azazel goat (Leviticus 16) and as one of the animals used for sacrifice for example for the atonement of sins. Goat idols could also refer to worship towards other gods (Leviticus 17:7).

In the New Testament, Christ uses the symbology of the goat as the opposite of the sheep. The sheep here symbolizes the righteous while the goat represents its antithesis. Since the sheep in this allegory refers to compassion and serving the community, the goat might here be understood as symbolizing egotism.

Matthew 25:31–46

When the Son of Man comes in his glory, and all the angels with him, he will sit on his glorious throne. All the nations will be gathered before him, and he will separate the people one from another as a shepherd separates the sheep from the goats. He will put the sheep on his right and the goats on his left.

Then the King will say to those on his right, 'Come, you who are blessed by my Father; take your inheritance, the kingdom prepared for you since the creation of the world. For I was hungry and you gave me something to eat, I was thirsty and you gave me something to drink, I was a stranger and you invited me in, I needed clothes and you clothed me, I was sick and you looked after me, I was in prison and you came to visit me.'

Then the righteous will answer him, 'Lord, when did we see you hungry and feed you, or thirsty and give you something to drink? When did we see you a stranger and invite you in, or needing clothes and clothe you? When did we see you sick or in prison and go to visit you?'

The King will reply, 'Truly I tell you, whatever you did for one of the least of these brothers and sisters of mine, you did for me.'

Then he will say to those on his left, 'Depart from me, you who are cursed, into the eternal fire prepared for the devil and his angels. For I was hungry and you gave me nothing to eat, I was thirsty and you gave me nothing to drink, I was a stranger and you did not invite me in, I needed clothes and you did not clothe me, I was sick and in prison and you did not look after me.'

They also will answer, 'Lord, when did we see you hungry or thirsty or a stranger or needing clothes or sick or in prison, and did not help you?'

"He will reply, 'Truly I tell you, whatever you did not do for one of the least of these, you did not do for me.'

Then they will go away to eternal punishment, but the righteous to eternal life."

Two of the most common symbolic features of the goat in different folklore are that it represents lust and determination/strong will.

Desire in itself, as we have mentioned in the chapter of the Dasa Mahavidyas, is also the driving force for personal will.

The goat is known for being strong-headed and stubborn. Compared with the sheep, it follows its own will more than that of the shepherd. God is often referred to as a shepherd in the Old Testament, and God's people are often referred to as sheep. In the New Testament, Christ refers to himself as the good shepherd. Christ talks about the sheep as the people who are his own and belong to God.

John 10:7–15

Therefore Jesus said again, "Very truly I tell you, I am the gate for the sheep. All who have come before me are

103

thieves and robbers, but the sheep have not listened to them. I am the gate; whoever enters through me will be saved. They will come in and go out, and find pasture. The thief comes only to steal and kill and destroy; I have come that they may have life, and have it to the full.

"I am the good shepherd. The good shepherd lays down his life for the sheep. The hired hand is not the shepherd and does not own the sheep. So when he sees the wolf coming, he abandons the sheep and runs away. Then the wolf attacks the flock and scatters it. The man runs away because he is a hired hand and cares nothing for the sheep.

"I am the good shepherd; I know my sheep and my sheep know me—just as the Father knows me and I know the Father—and I lay down my life for the sheep.

He contrasts those who belong to God with those who belong to the devil by who 'hears' the truth. The sheep listens to and follows the truth.

John 10:25–30

Jesus answered, "I did tell you, but you do not believe. The works I do in my Father's name testify about me, but you do not believe because you are not my sheep. My sheep listen to my voice; I know them, and they follow me. I give them eternal life, and they shall never perish; no one will snatch them out of my hand. My Father, who has given them to me, is greater than all; no one can snatch them out of my Father's hand. I and the Father are one."

John 8:42–47

Jesus said to them, "If God were your Father, you would love me, for I have come here from God. I have not come on my own; God sent me. Why is my language not clear to you? Because you are unable to hear what I say. You belong to your father, the devil, and you want to carry out your father's desires. He was a murderer from the beginning, not holding to the truth, for there is no truth in him. When he lies, he speaks his native language, for he is a liar and the father of lies. Yet because I tell the truth, you do not believe me! Can any of you prove me guilty of sin? If I am telling the truth, why don't you believe me? Whoever belongs to God hears what God says. The reason you do not hear is that you do not belong to God."

Sacrifice as Upholding Order, Truth and Showing Obedience to God

Christ also speaks of himself as laying down his life for his sheep.

John 10:14–18

"I am the good shepherd; I know my sheep and my sheep know me—just as the Father knows me and I know the Father—and I lay down my life for the sheep. I have other sheep that are not of this sheep pen. I must bring them also. They too will listen to my voice, and there shall be one flock and one shepherd. The reason my Father loves me is that I lay down my life—only to take it up again. No one takes it from

me, but I lay it down of my own accord. I have authority to lay it down and authority to take it up again. This command I received from my Father."

Luke 22:19–20

And he took bread, gave thanks and broke it, and gave it to them, saying, "This is my body given for you; do this in remembrance of me."

In the same way, after the supper, he took the cup, saying, "This cup is the new covenant in my blood, which is poured out for you.

Here, Christ talks of himself as a sacrificial animal giving his life to protect and gather his sheep and to give them life in abundance. In Isaiah, we find the obedient servant referred to as a sheep, maybe referring to the obedience of the servant.

Christ also speaks of his sacrifice as an act of obedience.

The Vedic sacrificial offering called yajna is a reciprocal act towards the gods/divine forces. It is an act upholding the relationship with the divine by giving to be able to receive. It was meant to create harmony/order in the form of a good relationship between humans and gods/divine forces, as well as between humans and the natural world.

The main aim was to uphold order and truth; rita. In the Vedic tradition, the outer sacrifice also became an inner sacrificial act with time.

The yasna of Zoroastrianism is related to the yajna of the Vedic tradition. The function of the yasna was to strengthen asha; order and truth.

In Judaism, the korban/sacrificial offering was also done to uphold a good relationship with God (YHWE).

We have mentioned the similarity between Belial meaning yokeless and yoga meaning yoked to God (Brahman) in the later Vedas. We have also discussed the symbology of the goat as driven by its own desire and will in contrast to the obedience of the sheep.

As we can see, the sacrificial offerings were meant to uphold order and truth as well as show obedience to that order and truth. We have also seen that this order was connected to life, in Zoroastrianism and in the Vedas. As we have seen, and will see, this connection between the underlying order and truth with life is also clear in the Bible.

Eternal Life

In Genesis with the fall of Eden, we can see that death was not a part of God's creation.

In the *Wisdom of Solomon*, usually dated to the first century BCE, it says that God didn't create death and that righteousness is deathless. Death was not seen as a part of creation but as something interfering with the perfect creation of God in the Judaic tradition.

Wisdom of Solomon says that death came into the world though the envy of the devil.

The *Wisdom of Solomon* also says that God formed us to be imperishable because we are made in the image of God's own nature.

Genesis 2:17 in Young's Literal translation says:

*and of the tree of knowledge of good and evil, thou dost
not eat of it, for in the day of thine eating of it--dying thou dost
die.'*

This literal translation of this verse points us to the process
of dying. The process we call ageing.

God is life, creates life and desires life. It is humans who
invite death.

Ezekiel 33:11

*Say to them, 'As surely as I live, declares the Sovereign
LORD, I take no pleasure in the death of the wicked, but rather
that they turn from their ways and live. Turn! Turn from your
evil ways! Why will you die, people of Israel?'*

Wisdom of Solomon 1:12–16, New American Bible (Revised Edition)

*Do not court death by your erring way of life,
nor draw to yourselves destruction by the works of your
hands.
Because God did not make death,
nor does he rejoice in the destruction of the living.
For he fashioned all things that they might have being,
and the creatures of the world are wholesome;
There is not a destructive drug among them,
nor any domain of Hades on earth,
For righteousness is undying.
It was the wicked who with hands and words invited
death,*

considered it a friend, and pined for it,
and made a covenant with it,
Because they deserve to be allied with it.

Christ often refers to people who we consider living as dead. Death is said to be invited by transgressions and sins.

Matthew 8:21–22

Another disciple said to him, "Lord, let me first go and bury my father."

But Jesus told him, "Follow me, and leave the dead to bury their own dead."

Ephesians 2:1–3

As for you, you were dead in your transgressions and sins, in which you used to live when you followed the ways of this world and of the ruler of the kingdom of the air, the spirit who is now at work in those who are disobedient. All of us also lived among them at one time, gratifying the cravings of our flesh and following its desires and thoughts. Like the rest, we were by nature deserving of wrath.

God is God of the living, and Christ says that he has come to give them life to the full. The 'full life' is eternal.

Matthew 22: 31–32

But about the resurrection of the dead—have you not read what God said to you, "I am the God of Abraham, the God of

Isaac, and the God of Jacob?" He is not the God of the dead but of the living.

John 10:10

The thief comes only to steal and kill and destroy; I have come that they may have life, and have it to the full.

John 3:16–17

For God so loved the world that he gave his one and only Son, that whoever believes in him shall not perish but have eternal life. For God did not send his Son into the world to condemn the world, but to save the world through him.

The word here is translated as 'only Son'; monogenes can also mean special or one-of-a-kind son.

The gospel, the good news of Christ is about the kingdom of God which is eternal life.

Luke 8:1

After this, Jesus traveled about from one town and village to another, proclaiming the good news of the kingdom of God. The Twelve were with him,

2 Timothy 1:10

but it has now been revealed through the appearance of our Savior, Christ Jesus, who has destroyed death and has brought life and immortality to light through the gospel.

Already in ancient Mesopotamia, the world's first civilization, immortality was a central theme of the main myths, as we have seen for example in the myth of Inanna.

Another of the central myths of ancient Mesopotamia was the myth of Adapa. This myth might have influenced the myth of the Garden of Eden since some of the themes are shared such as the gift of wisdom, the gift of immortality and being tricked into eating or not eating.

In this myth, Adapa, a man, rejects the food and water of life resulting in immortality offered to him by the god An. He does so because the god Enki has told him he would die if he ate anything offered. The god Enki had before this given Adapa the blessing of wisdom.

Ancient Egyptian religion was also centered around immortality and securing an eternal afterlife.

The Narrow Road That Leads to Life
Matthew 7:13–14

Enter through the narrow gate. For wide is the gate and broad is the road that leads to destruction, and many enter through it. But small is the gate and narrow the road that leads to life, and only a few find it.

John 10:7–9

Therefore, Jesus said again, "Very truly I tell you, I am the gate for the sheep. All who have come before me are thieves and robbers, but the sheep have not listened to them. I am the gate; whoever enters through me will be saved...

The road is to be followed whatever the cost, and whatever needs to be left behind.

Matthew 16:24–25

Then Jesus said to his disciples, "Whoever wants to be my disciple must deny themselves and take up their cross and follow me. For whoever wants to save their life will lose it, but whoever loses their life for me will find it.

Few will make this choice in this life.

Matthew 22:14, King James Version

For many are called, but few are chosen.

The path of order, truth and life is narrow and demands total obedience.

The Paths of the Righteous and the Unrighteous
Psalm 37:1–20

Do not fret because of those who are evil or be envious of those who do wrong;
for like the grass they will soon wither, like green plants, they will soon die away.
Trust in the LORD and do good;
dwell in the land and enjoy safe pasture.
Take delight in the LORD,

and he will give you the desires of your heart.

Commit your way to the LORD;

trust in him and he will do this:

He will make your righteous reward shine like the dawn, ⌈SEP⌉

your vindication like the noonday sun.

Be still before the LORD,

and wait patiently for him;

do not fret when people succeed in their ways when they carry out their wicked schemes.

Refrain from anger and turn from wrath; do not fret—it leads only to evil.

For those who are evil will be destroyed,

but those who hope in the LORD will inherit the land.

A little while, and the wicked will be no more;

though you look for them, they will not be found.

But the meek will inherit the land and enjoy peace and prosperity.

The wicked plot against the righteous and gnash their teeth at them;

but the LORD laughs at the wicked, for he knows their day is coming.

The wicked draw the sword and bend the bow to bring down the poor and needy, to slay those whose ways are upright.

But their swords will pierce their own hearts, and their bows will be broken.

Better the little that the righteous have than the wealth of many wicked;

for the power of the wicked will be broken, but the LORD upholds the righteous.

The blameless spend their days under the LORD's care, and their inheritance will endure forever.

In times of disaster, they will not wither; in days of famine, they will enjoy plenty.
But the wicked will perish:
Though the LORD's enemies are like the flowers of the field, they will be consumed, they will go up in smoke.

Wisdom of Solomon 2:1–24, New Revised Standard Version (Updated Edition)

For they reasoned unsoundly, saying to themselves,
Short and sorrowful is our life,
and there is no remedy when a life comes to its end,
and no one has been known to return from Hades.
For we were born by mere chance,
and hereafter we shall be as though we had never been, for the breath in our nostrils is smoke,
and reason is a spark kindled by the beating of our hearts; when it is extinguished, the body will turn to ashes, and the spirit will dissolve like empty air.
Our name will be forgotten in time, and no one will remember our works; our life will pass away like the traces of a cloud and be scattered like mist that is chased by the rays of the sun and overcome by its heat.
For our allotted time is the passing of a shadow, and there is no return from our death, because it is sealed up and no one turns back.
Come, therefore, let us enjoy the good things that exist and make use of the creation to the full as in youth.
Let us take our fill of costly wine and perfumes, and let no flower of spring pass us by.
Let us crown ourselves with rosebuds before they wither.

Let no meadow be free from our revelry; everywhere let us leave signs of enjoyment, because this is our portion, and this is our lot.

Let us oppress the righteous poor man; let us not spare the widow or regard the grey hairs of the aged.

But let our might be our law of right, for what is weak proves itself to be useless.

Let us lie in wait for the righteous man,

because he is inconvenient to us and opposes our actions; he reproaches us for sins against the law and accuses us of sins against our training.

He professes to have knowledge of God and calls himself a child of the Lord.

He became to us a reproof of our thoughts; the very sight of him is a burden to us,

because his manner of life is unlike that of others, and his ways are strange.

We are considered by him as something base, and he avoids our ways as unclean; he calls the last end of the righteous happy and boasts that God is his father.

Let us see if his words are true, and let us test what will happen at the end of his life,

for if the righteous man is God's child, he will help him[1] *and will deliver him from the hand of his adversaries.*

Let us test him with insult and torture, so that we may find out how reasonable he is and make a trial of his forbearance.

Let us condemn him to a shameful death, for, according to what he says, he will be protected.

Thus they reasoned, but they were led astray, for their wickedness blinded them,

115

and they did not know the secret purposes of God, nor hoped
for the wages of holiness, nor discerned the prize for
blameless souls,
for God created us for incorruption and made us in the image
of his own eternity,
but through an adversary's envy death entered the world, and
those who belong to his company experience it.

Here, we can see the connection between righteousness and eternal life and death and wickedness. We also see that the wicked use power to assert what is right and to oppress and test the righteous.

The righteous is seldom respected and cherished in this world. The pain that the righteous suffers is often misconstrued to be due to himself/herself even though it is the result of the oppression.

Isaiah 53: 2–5

... He had no beauty or majesty to attract us to him,
nothing in his appearance that we should desire him.
He was despised and rejected by mankind,
a man of suffering, and familiar with pain.
Like one from whom people hide their faces
he was despised, and we held him in low esteem.
Surely he took up our pain
and bore our suffering, yet we considered him punished by
God,
stricken by him, and afflicted.
But he was pierced for our transgressions,
he was crushed for our iniquities;

the punishment that brought us peace was on him…

But there is a reward which puts everything right.

Isaiah 53:10–11

Yet it was the LORD's will to crush him and cause him to suffer
and though the LORD makes his life an offering for sin, he will
see his offspring and prolong his days and the will of the LORD
will prosper in his hand.
After he has suffered,
he will see the light of life and be satisfied…

Matthew 5:3–12

"Blessed are the poor in spirit,
for theirs is the kingdom of heaven.
Blessed are those who mourn,
for they will be comforted.
Blessed are the meek,
for they will inherit the earth.
Blessed are those who hunger and thirst for righteousness, for
they will be filled.
Blessed are the merciful,
for they will be shown mercy.
Blessed are the pure in heart,
for they will see God.
Blessed are the peacemakers,
for they will be called children of God.
Blessed are those who are persecuted because of
righteousness,

for theirs is the kingdom of heaven.

Blessed are you when people insult you, persecute you and falsely say all kinds of evil against you because of me. Rejoice and be glad, because great is your reward in heaven, for in the same way they persecuted the prophets who were before you.

The people who are celebrated as righteous are not always the ones who are righteous.

Matthew 23:27–28

"Woe to you, teachers of the law and Pharisees, you hypocrites! You are like whitewashed tombs, which look beautiful on the outside but on the inside are full of the bones of the dead and everything unclean. In the same way, on the outside, you appear to people as righteous but on the inside you are full of hypocrisy and wickedness.

Forgiveness and Condemnation

There is both condemnation and punishment for sins described in the Bible as well as the possibility for forgiveness by repentance and turning from one's unrighteous ways.

Proverbs 28:13

Whoever conceals their sins does not prosper,
but the one who confesses and renounces them finds mercy.

For those who do not confess their sins and change their ways, there is punishment.

Matthew 23:13–15

"Woe to you, teachers of the law and Pharisees, you hypocrites! You shut the door of the kingdom of heaven in people's faces. You yourselves do not enter, nor will you let those enter who are trying to.

"Woe to you, teachers of the law and Pharisees, you hypocrites! You travel over land and sea to win a single convert, and when you have succeeded, you make them twice as much a child of hell as you are.

Matthew 23:29–36

"Woe to you, teachers of the law and Pharisees, you hypocrites! You build tombs for the prophets and decorate the graves of the righteous. And you say, 'If we had lived in the days of our ancestors, we would not have taken part with them in shedding the blood of the prophets.' So you testify against yourselves that you are the descendants of those who murdered the prophets. Go ahead, then, and complete what your ancestors started!

You snakes! You brood of vipers! How will you escape being condemned to hell? Therefore I am sending you prophets and sages and teachers. Some of them you will kill and crucify; others you will flog in your synagogues and pursue from town to town. And so upon you will come all the righteous blood that has been shed on earth, from the blood of righteous Abel to the blood of Zechariah son of Berekiah, whom you murdered between the temple and the altar. Truly I tell you, all this will come on this generation.

The condemnation is though not to be made by humans.

Matthew 5:43–45

"You have heard that it was said, 'Love your neighbor and hate your enemy.' But I tell you, love your enemies and pray for those who persecute you, that you may be children of your Father in heaven. He causes his sun to rise on the evil and the good, and sends rain on the righteous and the unrighteous.

Matthew 5:48

Be perfect, therefore, as your heavenly Father is perfect.

There will be rewards for good deeds.

Luke 6:35–36

But love your enemies, do good to them, and lend to them without expecting to get anything back. Then your reward will be great, and you will be children of the Most High because he is kind to the ungrateful and wicked. Be merciful, just as your Father is merciful.

Luke 6:37–38

"Do not judge, and you will not be judged. Do not condemn, and you will not be condemned. Forgive, and you will be forgiven. Give, and it will be given to you. A good measure, pressed down, shaken together and running over,

will be poured into your lap. For with the measure you use, it will be measured to you."

The reward will demand good deeds, not only lip service.

Luke 6:46–49

"Why do you call me, 'Lord, Lord', and do not do what I say? As for everyone who comes to me and hears my words and puts them into practice, I will show you what they are like. They are like a man building a house, who dug down deep and laid the foundation on rock. When a flood came, the torrent struck that house but could not shake it, because it was well-built. But the one who hears my words and does not put them into practice is like a man who built a house on the ground without a foundation. The moment the torrent struck that house, it collapsed and its destruction was complete."

Matthew 7:21

Not everyone who says to me, 'Lord, Lord', will enter the kingdom of heaven, but only the one who does the will of my Father who is in heaven.

The vengeance belongs not to humans but to God. Good deeds rewarded by evil will increase the punishment of that evil doing.

Matthew 26:24

The Son of Man will go just as it is written about him. But woe to that man who betrays the Son of Man! It would be better for him if he had not been born."

Romans 12:14–20

Bless those who persecute you; bless and do not curse. Rejoice with those who rejoice; mourn with those who mourn. Live in harmony with one another. Do not be proud, but be willing to associate with people of low position. Do not be conceited.

Do not repay anyone evil for evil. Be careful to do what is right in the eyes of everyone. If it is possible, as far as it depends on you, live at peace with everyone. Do not take revenge, my dear friends, but leave room for God's wrath, for it is written: "It is mine to avenge; I will repay," says the Lord. On the contrary:

If your enemy is hungry, feed him;
if he is thirsty, give him something to drink.
In doing this, you will heap burning coals on his head.'

Evil cannot be overcome by evil but only by good. Therefore, one should practice good. In that way, one conquer not only the evil without but also the evil within.

Romans 12:21

Do not be overcome by evil, but overcome evil with good.

In these texts, we see both the punishment and the possibility to repent and align with God, doing what is good. As we will see in the next chapter, goodness is being aligned with order, truth (righteousness) and love.

But didn't Christ take on the sins of others in his unjust death, freeing everyone from condemnation and death as long as we believe he is God's only Son?

Isaiah is believed to be one of the Scriptures in the Old Testament that Christ refers to when he says that something in his life needs to happen so that the Scriptures may be fulfilled.

Isaiah 53:7–12

He was oppressed and afflicted, yet he did not open his mouth; he was led like a lamb to the slaughter, and as a sheep, before its shearers is silent, so he did not open his mouth.

By oppression and judgment, he was taken away.

Yet who of his generation protested?

For he was cut off from the land of the living;

for the transgression of my people, he was punished.

He was assigned a grave with the wicked,

and with the rich in his death, though he had done no violence, nor was any deceit in his mouth.

Yet it was the LORD's will to crush him and cause him to suffer, and though the LORD makes his life an offering for sin, he will see his offspring and prolong his days, and the will of the LORD will prosper in his hand.

After he has suffered, he will see the light of life and be satisfied; by his knowledge, my righteous servant will justify many, and he will bear their iniquities.

123

Therefore, I will give him a portion among the great, and he will divide the spoils with the strong, because he poured out his life unto death, and was numbered with the transgressors.

For he bore the sin of many and made intercession for the transgressors.

This text is believed to prophesy about Christ. If we look at the text, we can see that the righteous servant of the Lord carries the sins of his people and bears their punishment. He also prayed for those who did him wrong.

In Luke 23:34, Christ says:

Jesus said, "Father, forgive them, for they do not know what they are doing..."

It is unclear if Christ asks for the forgiveness of everyone involved or for the people who have been unconsciously drawn into the power struggle of the authorities who have brought him to judgement and punishment to death.

In Isaiah 53, the righteous is rewarded for his action with a portion among the great. Nowhere here it is said that the offenders could escape their punishment without repenting and changing their ways.

Romans 12

Therefore, I urge you, brothers and sisters, in view of God's mercy, to offer your bodies as a living sacrifice, holy and pleasing to God—this is your true and proper worship.

Do not conform to the pattern of this world, but be transformed by the renewing of your mind. Then you will be able to test and approve what God's will is—his good, pleasing and perfect will.

If we compare this with the sayings of 'take your cross and follow me' as well as 'only the one who does the will of my Father will enter the kingdom of heaven', it becomes quite clear. The work has to be done by us all.

So then what was the work of Christ?

Isaiah 53:11

...by his knowledge, my righteous servant will justify many...

The work of Christ is to give eternal life by knowledge of God and to be an example of obedience to God for others to follow.

John 17:2–4

For you granted him authority over all people that he might give eternal life to all those you have given him. Now this is eternal life: that they know you, the only true God, and Jesus Christ, whom you have sent. I have brought you glory on earth by finishing the work you gave me to do.

Those who belong to God are called back to God and to eternal life.

John 17:6–9

"I have revealed you to those whom you gave me out of the world. They were yours; you gave them to me and they have obeyed your word. Now they know that everything you have given me comes from you. For I gave them the words you gave me, and they accepted them. They knew with certainty that I came from you, and they believed that you sent me. I pray for them. I am not praying for the world, but for those you have given me, for they are yours.

John 17:20

"My prayer is not for them alone. I pray also for those who will believe in me through their message,

Last Judgement

In Jewish eschatology, there is belief in a world to come (Olam ha-ba) that is not flawed and where the righteous are assured a place. This happens after a day of judgement (Yom ha-Din). A Messiah (anointed one) is believed to be ruling in this new world without evil.

In the New Testament, it is said about the end of the age:

Matthew 24:3

As Jesus was sitting on the Mount of Olives, the disciples came to him privately. "Tell us," they said, "when will this happen, and what will be the sign of your coming and of the end of the age?"

Matthew 24:7–14

Nation will rise against nation and kingdom against kingdom. There will be famines and earthquakes in various places. All these are the beginning of birth pains.

Then you will be handed over to be persecuted and put to death, and you will be hated by all nations because of me. At that time many will turn away from the faith and will betray and hate each other, and many false prophets will appear and deceive many people. Because of the increase of wickedness, the love of most will grow cold, but the one who stands firm to the end will be saved. And this gospel of the kingdom will be preached in the whole world as a testimony to all nations, and then the end will come.

As we can see here, Christ seems to talk about something far in the future. This 'gospel of the kingdom' will at that time have been spread around the world as a testimony to all nations.

It seems that the teaching of the Christ includes both an awakening of the dead to life, as we have seen referring to turning away from sin, and a last judgement.

John 5:25–29

Very truly I tell you, a time is coming and has now come when the dead will hear the voice of the Son of God and those who hear will live. For as the Father has life in himself, so he has granted the Son also to have life in himself. And he has given him authority to judge because he is the Son of Man. "Do not be amazed at this, for a time is coming when all who are in their graves will hear his voice and come out—those who have done what is good will rise to live, and those who have done what is evil will rise to be condemned.

The Christ explains what will condemn people.

John 12:47–50

"If anyone hears my words but does not keep them, I do not judge that person. For I did not come to judge the world, but to save the world. There is a judge for the one who rejects me and does not accept my words; the very words I have spoken will condemn them at the last day. For I did not speak on my own, but the Father who sent me commanded me to say all that I have spoken. I know that his command leads to eternal life. So whatever I say is just what the Father has told me to say."

The Christ also teaches about how the last judgment will be.

Matthew 25:31–46

"When the Son of Man comes in his glory, and all the angels with him, he will sit on his glorious throne. All the nations will be gathered before him, and he will separate the people one from another as a shepherd separates the sheep from the goats. He will put the sheep on his right and the goats on his left.

"Then the King will say to those on his right, 'Come, you who are blessed by my Father; take your inheritance, the

kingdom prepared for you since the creation of the world. For I was hungry and you gave me something to eat, I was thirsty and you gave me something to drink, I was a stranger and you invited me in, I needed clothes and you clothed me, I was sick and you looked after me, I was in prison and you came to visit me.'

"Then the righteous will answer him, 'Lord, when did we see you hungry and feed you, or thirsty and give you something to drink? When did we see you a stranger and invite you in, or needing clothes and clothe you? When did we see you sick or in prison and go to visit you?'

"The King will reply, 'Truly I tell you, whatever you did for one of the least of these brothers and sisters of mine, you did for me.'

"Then he will say to those on his left, 'Depart from me, you who are cursed, into the eternal fire prepared for the devil and his angels. For I was hungry and you gave me nothing to eat, I was thirsty and you gave me nothing to drink, I was a stranger and you did not invite me in, I needed clothes and you did not clothe me, I was sick and in prison and you did not look after me.'

"They also will answer, 'Lord, when did we see you hungry or thirsty or a stranger or needing clothes or sick or in prison, and did not help you?'

"He will reply, 'Truly I tell you, whatever you did not do for one of the least of these, you did not do for me.'

"Then they will go away to eternal punishment, but the righteous to eternal life."

As has been said, the Judaic notion of a last judgement and hell had probably been influenced by Zoroastrianism.

129

In Zoroastrianism, when a person dies, the soul is believed to stay close to the body for three days and three nights. This is an interesting parallel with the three days and three nights of Jona in the whale's stomach and of the Christ in death.

After this, according to Zoroastrianism, the soul continues to 'the Bridge of Judgement' where the person's righteousness is measured. If the person has been unrighteous, the bridge becomes more narrow, and the soul plunges into the world of Druj-Demana (House of Lies). In the House of Lies, the soul gets a fitting punishment for their deeds. If the person has been righteous, it is instead taken to the Garo-Demana (House of Songs). There is also a purgatory for those who are in equal doses righteous and unrighteous.

It is interesting to see the likeness between the narrow bridge of Zoroastrianism and the narrow road and gate that Christ talks about.

Judgement after death is not the ultimate end for the soul in Zoroastrianism. There is a last judgment when all the dead are resurrected and judged, after which the world is restored to goodness.

This last judgement starts with the awakening of the dead by a final savior of the world called Saoshyant. This figure of Zoroastrianism is believed to be a predecessor of the messianic figure of Judaism. The Saoshyant is said to be born by a virgin, as Christ was claimed to be.

After the awakening of the dead, all have to walk through molten metal which purifies the unrighteous completely. This purification by molten metal creates a new body for the individual and all becomes immortal.

This will be the ultimate restoration of the world to goodness according to Zoroastrianism.

According to the creation myth of Zoroastrianism, God/Ahura Mazda created the material world to ensnare evil and defeat it by this process.

Still, it is hard not to wonder why there is a need for two judgements.

One possible explanation is reincarnation. This is not part of Zoroastrianism but it would explain the need for two judgments. In that case, every life could be seen as part of the purification process with one judgement after each individual death and then a last judgement that installs goodness as the rule of the universe.

As we have seen Zoroastrianism and the Vedic tradition are related and in the Vedic tradition, reincarnation is a concept introduced in the early Upanishads. In the Brihadaranyaka (about 600–900 BCE), the law of karma and reincarnation are described.

Ancient Egypt is a term referring to the early civilization of Egypt and is said to have begun around 3000 BCE. The religious beliefs of the early Egyptian civilization included belief in an underworld, judgment of the individual and an eternal ideal afterlife in a paradisiac milieu. These beliefs of ancient Egypt predate those of Zoroastrianism and Abrahamic religion.

In ancient Egyptian religion, it was believed that all common people had to pass through the underworld after death. Here, they were challenged to be able to pass different forms of guardian deities.

After this, they reached 'the Judgement of the dead'. The deceased's heart was weighed against the feather of the goddess Maát. The feather of Maát represents truth and justice. If the heart weighed more than the feather, the deceased's heart was devoured by the goddess Ammit leaving them eternally restless. They were after this trapped in the underworld: Duat. Their existence was a state of nonbeing and chaos since they had gone against the order of life, both cosmic and social, called maát.

The unrighteous who had not lived according to maát had to dwell in the underworld without the reviving light of the sun god Re. They were condemned to total darkness.

They were seen as the children of the god Seth who brought death into the world by murdering his brother, the god Osiris. Interesting to compare with the story of Cain and Abel in the Old Testament.

The righteous were instead brought to immortality and an ideal afterlife. The paradisiac milieu where these deceased were brought was called Sekhet-Aaru. Here, they could communicate with gods and passed on loved ones through thoughts.

It is very interesting to see the similarities of this with what near-death experiencers from different cultures and religions describe today about coming sometimes to a hellish place (a dark place of punishment), sometimes passing through this to a paradisiac place, or coming directly to a paradisiac place and often meeting passed loved ones. There is also often testimony about communication happening through means of thoughts. Many report songs in the air being emitted from all things (compare with the House of Songs) and a feeling of being united with everything and feeling love for everything/everyone and from everything/everyone. Many describe being confronted with the consequences of their actions, some of them experiencing being shown transmigration.

One may wonder if the ground for religious beliefs comes from people who have had these forms of experiences. In Vedic tradition the people who were the source of the knowledge of the Veda were the rishis; the 'seers'. The Judaic tradition had its prophets. The nature religions had their shamans. The mystical traditions had their mystics.

Unity

Jesus talked about love. This seems to be connected to an underlying unity.

It is interesting to note the similarity with the remembrance of the experience of unity and compassion leading to the awakening of the Buddha, and the description of the Buddha awakening together with all creatures.

John 15:9

"As the Father has loved me, so have I loved you. Now remain in my love.

John 17:20–23

"My prayer is not for them alone. I pray also for those who will believe in me through their message, that all of them may be one, Father, just as you are in me and I am in you. May they also be in us so that the world may believe that you have sent me. I have given them the glory that you gave me, that they may be one as we are one—I in them and you in me— so that they may be brought to complete unity. Then the world

will know that you sent me and have loved them even as you have loved me.

John 15:12

My command is this: Love each other as I have loved you.

John 15:17

This is my command: Love each other.

Evil is connected by Christ to egotism and self-serving behavior, the opposite of love and unity. What Christ talks about here is of course built on the commandments of the Judaic tradition.

Mark 7:20–23

He went on: "What comes out of a person is what defiles them. For it is from within, out of a person's heart, that evil thoughts come—sexual immorality, theft, murder, adultery, greed, malice, deceit, lewdness, envy, slander, arrogance and folly. All these evils come from inside and defile a person."

Evil is connected to death and untruth.

John 8:44

You belong to your father, the devil, and you want to carry out your father's desires. He was a murderer from the beginning, not holding to the truth, for there is no truth in him.

When he lies, he speaks his native language, for he is a liar and the father of lies.

As we have seen in the teaching of Christ, in Zoroastrianism and in Vedic tradition there is an order of truth and life as opposed to untruth and death.

Righteousness and love is described as the way to eternal life. As we have seen righteousness is connected to doing what upholds the order of truth and life.

1 John 3:10

This is how we know who the children of God are and who the children of the devil are: Anyone who does not do what is right is not God's child, nor is anyone who does not love their brother and sister.

1 John 3:11–15

For this is the message you heard from the beginning: We should love one another. Do not be like Cain, who belonged to the evil one and murdered his brother. And why did he murder him? Because his own actions were evil and his brothers were righteous. Do not be surprised, my brothers and sisters, if the world hates you. We know that we have passed from death to life because we love each other. Anyone who does not love remains in death. Anyone who hates a brother or sister is a murderer, and you know that no murderer has eternal life residing in him.

The Serpent Power

The serpent is one of the oldest and most commonly used mythological symbols.

Serpents live close to the ground and shed their skins and are therefore connected to the earth and the regeneration of life.

The Hopi people performed an annual snake dance to renew the fertility of nature.

This happened through the union of Snake Youth (sky spirit) and Snake Girl (underworld spirit). The description is interestingly similar to the idea of uniting upper and lower Kundalini.

In their connection to fertility, serpents are connected to sexuality.

In the biblical story of the fall from Eden, the serpent may therefore be connected to sexuality and desire. In the tantric tradition, iccha is connected to both desire and will since desire is what creates the foundation for personal will. The Tree of Knowledge is said in the story to give knowledge of good and evil, making the human as the gods. This may be understood as the human making his/her own decisions, and exercising free will.

The serpent has also sometimes become connected to immortality.

In the ancient Mesopotamian epic of Gilgamesh, a snake steals Gilgamesh's plant of rejuvenation. This is similar to the story of the fall from Eden when Adam and Eve are prevented from eating from the Tree of Life (which gives immortality) after the serpent has tricked them into eating from the Tree of Knowledge.

Several Mesopotamian myths are considered to have influenced stories in the Old Testament, such as the Great Flood and the story of the Garden of Eden. Both of these stories are connected to eternal life in the Mesopotamian versions.

In the story of the Great Flood, the man and wife, rescued by the god Enki by asking them to build a boat and take with them their family and the animals of the fields, are rewarded after the flood with eternal life. In the epic of Gilgamesh, the man saved from the flood tells Gilgamesh, who wishes for eternal life, about a plant of rejuvenation at the bottom of the sea. The plant is found by Gilgamesh but then gets stolen by a serpent. An interesting part of this myth is that the serpent sheds its skin as it departs with the stolen plant. The capacity of the serpent to shed its skin is a reason why it has been connected to immortality.

In the gospel of John, Christ uses the symbology of the snake as a symbology of a vertical movement leading to eternal life.

John 3:14–15

Just as Moses lifted up the snake in the wilderness, so the Son of Man must be lifted up, that everyone who believes may have eternal life in him.

John 12:32

And I, when I am lifted up from the earth, will draw all people to myself."

The Mayans communicated with their ancestors through a Vision Serpent. The Vision Serpent was connected to a mythical World Tree which created a vertical axis between the spiritual and earth planes.

The upright cobra was used as a symbol of divine authority in ancient Egypt on the head ornaments of the pharaohs.

Buddha is often depicted with the naga (serpent being) Mucalinda ascending behind Buddha with his many heads above the head of Buddha.

Quetzalcoatl, a deity depicted as a feathered serpent was one of the main Mesoamerican deities.

A stone carving dated to around 900 BC is the earliest Mesoamerican depiction of a feathered serpent, The carving depicts a serpent rising up behind a person seemingly engaged in shamanic ritual.

It is interesting to see the two elements of feathers (usually connected to creatures of the sky) and serpents (usually connected to the earth), coexisting in this deity. Especially since the shaman in all cultures has been seen as the connecting bridge between the worlds, often in the form of heaven and earth and the underworld.

Quetzalcoatl was connected to Venus and to death and resurrection (compare with Inanna). It was said in one of his myths that he created humans of this age from the bones of the humans of the age before, together with his own blood. He was especially connected to Venus as the morning star. One of his titles Tlahuizcalpantecuhtli means 'lord of the star of the dawn'.

Another of his myths relates to his connection to Venus. In this myth, he was said to have gotten drunk and engaged in a sexual act with his sister who was a celibate priestess. In shame, he thereafter set himself on fire (probably as a self-sacrificial act) and with the smoke, his heart followed to the sky and became the morning star.

The name Quetzalcoatl comes from the words, quetzal (an emerald plumed bird) and coatl (serpent). In one of his myths, he is said to have been born by a virgin who swallowed an emerald.

Emerald green as we have seen is also a color connected to the goddess Matangi and the word made manifest through desire. Quetzalcoatl and Matangi seem connected to desire both as a destructive force and a liberating force if we look at the symbology of the myth of Quetzalcoatl above and at how Matangi is described.

Another interesting similarity between Quetzalcoatl and Matangi is that they are both connected to spiral shells. Quetzalcoatl is connected to the wind. This may also be the case with Matangi as she might represent vayu/Prana (vital wind) as desire turned towards the world or returning to the source.

Serpents have also been associated with venom and medicine. In the Bible, Moses erects a bronze serpent on a pole as protection from venomous serpents (Numbers 21:4–9).

The symbology of serpents as healing is also found in the rod of Asclepius (a Greek god), a staff entwined by one serpent, representing healing and medicine.

In the ancient Indian myth, Samudra Manthana; "Churning of the ocean of milk," the king of the serpents Vasuki is used as a churning rope. In some versions of the myth, this makes Vasuki vomit his poison; in other versions of the myth, the poison is said to rise from the ocean. In both versions, Shiva takes the poison in his throat to control it, which makes his throat turn blue.

If we compare this with what is said about the throat in the chakra system given, Visuddhi is said to be the place where the poison (the cycle of death and rebirth; samsara) and the nectar of immortality are held. It is the place of completion, the place where the physical reemerges into the non-physical. Here nature's cycle of death and rebirth (samsara) may be transcended.

Amrita is said to be both poison and nectar of immortality the same way as Kundalini is said to bind us to the transient world and to liberate us from it. The poison here might be understood as the binding face of Kundalini (that binds us into samsara) and the nectar as the liberating face of Kundalini that liberates us from samsara. The religious scholar Lilian Silburn has found in her research that Kundalini is described as poison in her unliberated state and as nectar of immortality in her liberated state. This is similar to the dual role of the serpent as venom and medicine.

In the tantric tradition, desire and will is understood to be the power binding us to the transient world as well as the power that brings us back 'home' to what is eternal. This process is the process of Kundalini and is probably described in the symbology of the Mahavidyas. Some of the Mahavidyas are depicted with snakes.

In the fall from Eden, the serpent may symbolize the binding to transient life (life and death). As Christ uses the symbology of the vertical movement/lifting of the serpent as leading to eternal life, this might point to the liberating part of the symbology of the serpent.

Shiva's blue throat may symbolize the liberated energy transformed from poison to nectar. (See Vishuddhi and Ajna under 'Chakras')

Shiva in imagery carries the serpent king Vasuki around his neck making the connection between the serpent and the dual function of amrita as nectar and poison even more plausible, since the myth of 'Samudra Manthana' (The churning of the ocean of milk) is often understood as a symbology of the yogic process. And Shiva is considered the lord of yoga.

All this said, Kundalini according to the religious scholars Wallis and Tompkins is not described as a serpent power in the Tantras. The serpent is only used as a simile, among others.

Even so, one might wonder if it is a coincidence that a symbol so widely used for fertility, desire, earth, cycles of nature, venom, medicine, and immortality is attached to Kundalini seemingly symbolizing the exact same things.

My Life as a Mystic

Childhood

I grew up Christian. My mother was the one with the stronger faith. My parents were not church-going people but my mother always used to pray with us children before going to sleep. My mother's faith had gotten stronger after a car accident where my parents lost a son before I was born. My mother also lost her father in that accident. My mother prayed desperately to know that my brother was with her father after the accident. One evening when they watched TV, she saw her father entering the living room.

I was a sensitive child. I was especially afraid of the dark. I used to imagine angels standing around my bed as protection, to be able to sleep. One night, when I was 5 years old, I had a very real dream. A very tall lady made of white light, seemingly floating above the floor, came to my bed to wake me up. She said without using her lips to follow her. I felt she was benign, so I was not afraid. She took me to a cave. There were others like her there but she was the leader. She 'said' that I was one of them and that I was never alone. They were always with me.

As a child, I always asked my parents the big questions they couldn't answer. When I was old enough to read my own books, I started going to the library to loan books on all spiritual topics I could find. I was also interested in old cultures. The first book I remember borrowing from the library on my own was called *Tulku*. It was about the search for the reincarnation of a lama who had passed. I didn't believe in reincarnation though. I was a devout Christian.

Even so, in hindsight, I can see that some of my favorite things that I used to play as a child maybe weren't that common to children at large.

One of my favorites was playing a wise woman blending potions in the forest close to my home.

I loved playing that I was from different cultures, imitating the way they dressed, pretending to live in their way of life.

I used to love sitting by the window to look at the stars. I started writing poetry at 6–7 years of age.

At the age of about 11–12, I saw a film about a nun who would lie face down in a cross formation according to her order. After that, I used to do this when I thought no one was watching. I don't know why this appealed to me so much. It just felt right.

When I was 12, I started meditating from examples in the books. I also did some things I hadn't read. One thing I would do was stare at the mirror into my eyes until my face started shifting. It shifted between men and women of different ages, from different cultures to a skeleton to disappearing. I always felt I had a special way of looking when I did this. I was fascinated but also scared.

I was always tortured by the knowledge of the suffering of others, all over the world, as early as I can remember.

Teenage Years

From the age of 13, I started to have very vivid dreams.

At the age of 13, I dreamt that I was in a spaceship. The spaceship worked as a hang glider. It generated speed and then it glided until it was out of speed. With this, I had to fly from one planet to the next in some sort of planetary system. I had to do this to save the world. It was clear in the dream that only I could do it. Praying desperately to God for help, while gliding between the planets not knowing if I would fall down in-between into infinite space, I jumped from planet to planet. Before reaching the last planet, I think I fell down. I woke up with a quaffed scream, 'Adonai'. I wrote it down and hoped I would get an answer to what it meant at some point. I took a chance and looked it up in an encyclopedia. The Internet did not yet exist. To my surprise, I found it. It meant 'my lord' in Hebrew. To my knowledge, I had not been in contact with that word before.

During these years, I sometimes had dreams about an older Native American woman who came to tell me things. I remember especially one dream when I tried to run away from her, but wherever I ran, she was in front of me. What she told me in the dream happened afterwards, even things far in the future.

I often had a feeling that I had left my body at night to do some kind of work to help others. My sister told me later that she often found me sitting up in bed in the night with my eyes wide open, sleeping. I often woke up in a sitting position during this period. It felt as if a part of me had been guarding my body.

I sometimes practiced to get out of my body. I had developed this practice on my own. I had gotten the idea

145

(probably from church) that people like me would become persecuted and probably tortured, and since I didn't think I would be able to handle torture, I would need to learn how to escape the body. In my practice, I would come to a point where my head felt really stuffed.

This time something changed. I remember a feeling of being pulled from the backside of my head. I then felt something like a drum inside my body. I don't know if it was my heart. It continued to get stronger and faster. At some point, it became too strong to stop. It became harder and faster until I felt my body would soon not be able to take it anymore. I felt I was going to die. Just then, it stopped. Perfect stillness. Then I realized I was seeing the ceiling very close to my face. I thought something like: *How can I get out of here*? Then I was in the sky, among the stars. I thought: *How can this help anybody*? and I returned to my body again.

Once or twice after this, I might have had out-of-body experiences, I turned as I slept but my body didn't follow; once I experienced falling down to the floor but my body didn't follow.

I had all sorts of spiritual experiences from the age of 14 to 20. I saw auras around people and around non-living things. I could lean into an energy that moved instead of me. When I was 19, I was tired of all the strange things happening. I was tired of not getting enough real sleep. Tired of being afraid.

I turned to the spiritual teachers in my city for help to make it stop. They said that they couldn't help. Only one spiritual couple said that maybe if I learned to channel the energy, I could learn how to control it. They also worked with angels. They taught me Reiki but they soon discovered that I was using what they called Psychic healing naturally and that

that was stronger, so they encouraged me to continue with that. I saw the people around me as bodies of light when I did it.

One day, when I was 20, after having a feeling all day of extreme well-being, love and safety, I slept at a friend's house, a new place for me. We arrived when it was dark.

In the morning, I seemingly woke up. I saw the room in daylight. A woman passed my bed and walked to the window. She was made of white yellowish light. She seemed to be of medium height. She knew I was watching. She turned her face so I could see her eye. It was black and big and almond-shaped like an alien. I started to panic. I could feel the pull in the back of my head as I did in the experience at 13.

My friend and her boyfriend who had slept at the same place came to calm me down. It worked until I realized I was looking two ways at the same time and none of them in the direction of how my face was turned. I started to panic again. I heard the paws of what I imagined to be a bulldog ready to attack. I used all my force to pull myself out of the tornado in the back of my head.

Grown Up Years

From the age of 21–28, I concentrated on earthly things. I felt a need to do practical work for the world.

First, I became a social worker. I did my field practice for a term in India when I was 21 years old. I worked with street children and their families. I had no previous connections to India and it wasn't my first choice to go there. I went because a fellow student found out that we could work with street theatre at an NGO there.

Actually, I was afraid to go since at this time, the vulnerability of poverty was what plagued me the most. Nearing the end of my fieldwork practice, I had a dream. In the dream, I was dancing with a very old and very poor woman. In the dream, I had a strong orgasmic experience. Later when learning of the Mahavidyas, I thought of this as a meeting with the aspect of Dhumavati.

After my social work studies, I continued to study to become a psychotherapist. I wanted to understand the depth of the psyche and how to help people heal from trauma. I also wanted to understand my experiences.

Dance have also been of great importance to me. I danced from when I was 3 years old. For 10 years, I practiced a form of Indian classical dance; Odissi. I started practicing this dance form after a feeling when first encountering it as an old memory.

At the age of 29 in 2005, I moved to Beijing, China with my husband. My goal was to study dance, but when that didn't work out the way I had planned, I prayed for guidance and ended up at a yoga school. I studied yoga for a year, and I continued my daily practice after this.

I had been in contact with the yogic tradition since I lived in India in 1998, but this encounter of yoga with my teacher Mohan was that of pure white light entering my body, and I knew this was the path for me to follow.

My strongest experiences of white light before had been sitting meditation in Matrimandir in Auroville (Sri Aurobindo and the French mother's place) during the weekends in India. The white light was deeply present there, but the difference was that in sitting meditation, it didn't seem to integrate with the body as efficiently.

For a period of time, I studied at Kaivalyadhama in India, partially with O.P. Tiwari.

One day when walking towards him to class in the early morning, he said to me, "Ah, here comes Maria the Great." I didn't know what he was talking about, so I asked. He said, "Do you really not know?"

I responded, "No."

He said, "Then maybe that is for the best."

From the age of 33–36, I had my children.

A Calling From Above

When I was 37, I was standing in the shower when a yellow light, like the sun filled my head. I heard the word 'Trisundari' over and over again. I didn't know what it meant. An old social worker colleague of mine in India had been called Sundar so I knew that meant 'shining'. Tri I knew meant three since I danced classical Indian dance and practiced yoga.

I asked a friend if she recognized the word. She said it sounded like the name of a specific goddess. She looked her up and found her name to be Tripurasundari.

My friend told me about Sally Kempton and her book *Awakening Shakti* and about her connection to the lineage referred to in the book *Eat, Love, Pray* by Elizabeth Gilbert. Embarrassed I had been reading that book several times in a row during that spring, I didn't want to read anything else, but I had no idea why. This was in 2014.

In the spring of 2015, I attended a pranayama workshop with my old teacher from Kaivalyadhama Sri OP Tiwari and his son Sudhir Tiwari. I talked to Sudhir Tiwari about my progress and he gave me a practice in response. It was a sort of belly pump being done for a couple of days. I also got a mantra practice and a pranayama practice.

Later that spring, I attended a week-long meditation teacher training with Sally Kempton from the Siddha Yoga lineage, Muktananda's lineage.

The day before the training I felt a very strong (double-edged) energy. The energy field was so strong that I couldn't fall asleep for several hours.

Being in this in-between state between being asleep and awake, a very colorful and bright picture came to me. The picture was large and coming from a distance. It was something like a kaleidoscope of moving tigers. Every time I started to sink into relaxation, the picture returned.

When almost falling asleep, I was woken up by a very alive image of snakes (maybe 6 or 8) joined at the tail, all hissing at me. This happened about 3 to 4 times. Then I finally fell asleep. The morning after I woke up with pressure in the middle of the forehead, over the root of the nose and in my eyes.

During the training, I asked Sally Kempton for some of her time and told her about my spiritual history since childhood. She decided from this to give me a mantra from her tradition with the intention for it to carry her lineage transmission.

I practice for a period of time the mantra from Sudhir Tiwari, Kaivalyadhama and the enlivened mantra from Sally Kempton.

First, I started to experience a sensation like I was being lifted. I started to feel like floating in the air. It felt so real that I got afraid that I would be lifted from my seat. This came back stronger and stronger.

One night, right after the workshop, when this first happened during mantra practice, I was given as a gift the word 'madya' in a dream. This is how it was explained in the dream, as a gift. Today I know that this word refers to the central channel (Shushumna) and the state beyond duality, but I didn't know that then.

I started to see two 'me' with my inner vision, looking the same, one inside the other. I experienced something very clear breaking through my vision. I also had this quality of crystal-clear sight sometimes during the day. In meditation, I started to experience work being done on one eye per meditation.

One day after mantra practice, I heard the sound of burning wood at the top of my head. The day after, the energy moved so quickly and so effortlessly through the body with the mantra that I couldn't keep pace with it. I had to let it repeat itself energetically after a while.

I went through a period when I experienced a lot of energy work in the throat, the palette, and from there a vibration in the center of the head (Ajna).

I went through a phase of experiencing a feeling of 'digging' in the head while reciting my mantras.

One night when practicing, something forceful made me say inside, "Lakshmi, Saraswati, Parvati, Shiva." Then I saw Ganesha with my inner eye. Then even stronger 'Shiva' was said through me again.

After this meditation during the night, I dreamt. In the 'dream', I seemed to wake up.

I was in the room where I slept, it was pretty dark but not fully. I woke up by somebody breathing warm air on my cheek. I looked up and above me, I saw Muktananda's face. We communicated but not through the mouth. He seemed to be there to check me out. He took a good look at me, then he said, "You are younger than I thought."

In the morning when I woke up, my children had ripped apart my mala that I had practiced my mantras with.

I contacted Sally Kempton about the experience since I guessed the experience was connected to the transmission she intendedly gave me. I learned that the breaking of the mala signified the breaking of certain karmas and that mantras were said to dissolve hidden karmas in the subtle body.

After this, the mantras given by Sally Kempton and Sudhir Tiwari felt dead. I tried to repeat them for some more time but then I let go of the practice.

I continued to practice the pranayama practice described by Sudhir Tiwari.

With my inner eye, I saw a strong yellow light filling and shining from my body in relaxation. After practice, I often saw a strong color of dark sapphire blue. I started to see sparks of sapphire blue light with my eyes closed and open sometimes during and after practice.

During one meditation, I saw the dark sapphire blue in a round shape above my eyebrows with my eyes closed and open. It was surrounded by a yellow halo. I remembered that I had seen it before.

I read Yogananda and found that he called this 'Christ Consciousness'. Another time, I saw it as having a small flat edge on top.

I had an old inner struggle with Christ. I felt he didn't think I was a good enough person, that he would judge me to hell. I talked to Christ inside. I was angry and frustrated about feeling that his demands on me were not something that I could live up to.

Then I 'heard' inside; "I love you. I don't want you any harm."

I felt for the first time in my life that Christ was not angry with me.

During one meditation after this, I saw with my inner eye a gestalt above my eyebrows filled with yellow light and with a lot of yellow light shining from it. It was Christ. I heard 'savior'. Then I turned into Christ. Then I felt like I was getting bigger in the form of Christ.

I started to see energy around my limbs with my open eyes when practicing as lightning-like sparks. I heard and felt the energy increasing during practice and turn into a strong white light filling me.

One night, I woke up from a very strong buzzing from the nerves of the eyes to Ajna and from there up to a point at the center top of my head. They felt like laser beams. It was extremely forceful, but I tried to trust the process.

I started doing Shambavi Mudra with some asana. I also felt drawn to doing tantric simple Kechari Mudra which I had never felt drawn to before.

I also felt compelled to roll my head up and down with the breath in Ardha Pashimottanasana with Shambavi mudra. I found it later in a book from Satyananda as a kriya form of Maha mudra.

In the late summer of 2016, I saw a strong yellowish-white light fill my head from the body in meditation. Later that night, I woke up from a sonic boom that seemed to come from the top of my head. The feeling was as if falling upwards.

In the autumn of 2016, I met two teachers. One was an Indonesian shaman, who had clinically died and came back to life with new abilities. One was a tantric teacher. The Indonesian shaman, together with a Balinese shaman, gave me an energetic cleansing. I just told about my spiritual background to the tantric teacher.

The tantric teacher thought that I had gone long in my process and was unsure if she could do anything for me. I said I got the feeling she had gone one step further in allowing this force in than me and that I felt hindered by fear but remembered my courage and trust when sensing hers.

During a period of time, much focus was placed on Manipura in my practice. The focus was not placed by me but came spontaneously.

Once in meditation after pranayama practice, I saw the energy in me as a dark form of plasma with colors inside, as a space. I felt a vast stillness. I felt a broadening of my awareness. I heard people chanting in what sounded like Sanskrit. I could distinguish the word 'Brihaspati.' Brihaspati is the force/god dispelling the darkness and bringing in the light. It is associated with the planet Jupiter and the principle of the guru.

In the beginning of 2017, I dreamt that I got bitten by a snake at the backside of my heart, between my shoulder blades. I was before and after this time tormented by thoughts and feelings and dreams about the sexual abuse of children.

In the summer of 2017, the Indonesian teacher gave me an initiation to contact the angelic realm. This process was extremely energetically intense, even though the only thing I did was to expose myself to a yantra and a mantra a couple of minutes once a week for 11 weeks. Later I learned that these were from a channel named Astrea Sri Ana.

The initiations resulted in a message in a dream. It was the first night of Navaratri 21 September 2017. An older woman looking mixed Indian and Native American said to me, "You are Venus because you have no desire, but don't tell anyone. The fire will consume what is needed bit by bit as you meet it."

I had a session after the initiation with the Indonesian teacher. I was focused on telling her about the dream.

She asked me if I had received a message from the angels after the initiations. I said no. No recollection of the dream was there. After the session was over, the memory returned directly. I remembered what was said; "Don't tell anyone."

The process afterwards brought up extreme amounts of dirt. I was confronted with problems with parasites; intestinal worms and bugs in our entire kitchen. The world changed so I could only see the broken, the downtrodden.

The things most painful for me in the suffering of the world got closer and closer. My practice and prayers for the world became more and more desperate. The process was for about seven months. It ended with me getting into the hospital from a parasite (from earlier times in India) that had stuck to my liver. This happened in the beginning of 2018.

An Answer From Below

In the summer of 2018, I was booked into a retreat with the tantric teacher. I had met her twice at this time to talk about my spiritual process, but I had never engaged in any form of practice or ritual with her. I wasn't sure if I should go because of my health.

We decided I would join but take it very easy. I did. I didn't attend anything more than evening talks and food times. The rest of the time, I lay in my room and rested, having a feeling like floating, even when lying down, that wouldn't go away. It felt related to my neck.

One evening, we were to have a fire ritual. I was to offer something up. We had discussed in the group before what we wanted to offer. I said, "I have nothing more to give, I have given too much." I was depleted. All my energy had for such a long time been consumed by the torture of the suffering of the world, and no veil to protect me.

I was proposed to offer the offering up.

At this time in 2018 at the ritual, I had had a 14-year-long daily practice of yoga; asana, pranayama, meditation and mantra.

I had received a calming, healing mantra from the tantric teacher during the day 'Som'. As I was practicing it, I started to hear the vibration and feel the energy of the mantra in the body as I often did at this time.

I started to ask questions in my head. I wondered why I was not getting well, if I was doing something wrong, if I had work left to do, or if I was not worthy to get well. Then I thought, *No I have worked enough, I just want to get well and to be with my family, and take care of my children. I don't care about spiritual experiences or enlightenment anymore.* Then I heard, "Ok, let's take it away." It sounded like a leader talking to a group of fellow workers.

I think it started at the ritual with the blue sparks when I closed my eyes, but I didn't pay much attention to them. It was actually more like the same spark being in many places at the same time.

I guess we must have already done our offering with our mantra in the fire ritual. It was a mantra for liberation that was

156

familiar to me, connected to it a power mantra associated with the goddess Tripurasundari, but I didn't know that at the time.

Then one of the people around the fire, a close disciple of the teacher, had some kind of reaction. To my eyes, it looked psychological and the teacher and the group had everything under control, so I decided to leave the circle so as not to waste any of my very sparse energy.

There were some tones coming through me but I didn't think much of it.

The close disciple of the teacher was now back in the circle sitting close to me. I reached out in love and support and I felt a strong electric energy coming from his hand into mine. I let it flow through my hand and into the fire, not to push my system in any way.

At some point, I felt jolts through my body and my arms moved upwards. I was used to bodily kriyas (involuntary movements and sounds) from my yoga practice so I didn't think much of that either. It was not forceful so I could easily hold them back. There were now letters coming through me; ab, ad, am. I thought it sounded like primal sounds, the kind babies do.

We were asked by the teacher to take each other's hands in the circle around the fire, so I made a quick decision to stay. I didn't expect anything special to happen.

Almost directly I felt an energy wave from the teacher being sent around the circle. After just a couple of circulations, I felt the energy was so strong in me that I soon would not be able to control it.

I shouted, "Stop, stop. I'm losing control."

The teacher said, "It's ok. I'm not afraid of you." Actually, she said 'afraid for you' but I misheard.

I said, "I'm not afraid of me either. I'm afraid of it (the energy). Can it be too strong? Can it hurt me?"

The teacher looked me in the eyes and said, "No."

I said, "Are you sure?"

She said, "I'm sure." I decided to trust and let it continue. In a couple of seconds, my body was shaking violently. My chest was being pulled up repeatedly.

Then my pelvic floor started to contract. I had given birth twice at that time, and this felt similar. The only difference was that the body pushed upwards with immense force instead of downwards as in labour. The energy seemed to exit my scull in a fan shape, extremely forcefully.

The contractions had the same pattern as in labour. It went to a climax and then receded. Those who held my hands said I tensed forcefully with every contraction.

When I lost control and the first contraction came, my body screamed 'Amma'. It happened with every contraction. The sound of my voice was so desperate and there was a part of me witnessing the process that became so sad hearing this, that it sobbed for me in the pauses between the contractions. The contractions became more and more forceful.

In the same way, as in one of my labours, I felt I was not going to survive if it continued, but just as in labour, I had no control over it. When I had passed what I thought was my utmost limit, it started to wind down. I shook violently afterwards and my whole body was still shaking as I was helped to my room by two people from the circle.

The whole night I was vibrating. I was not really asleep nor not really awake. In this state, I saw a newborn baby. I wondered if this might be another child that I would get since I had seen both of my children this way before I conceived.

Someone was carrying the baby towards me and as it came close, I "heard," "Let us present, Maria." I understood that it was me.

During that spring I had a thought in my mind that maybe my birth name Maria wasn't the right name for me anymore. The day I asked for guidance with my new name, I went to work as usual, and on the tram later that day, a beggar asked me for some money, which I gave. He left, then stopped to look for something among his belongings and came back with a picture of Mary (Maria) and Christ.

Burning Up

For months after I was burning up, I lay in bed for weeks with cold wet towels around me. My whole body had a constant extreme buzzing inside. It felt as if it was my nerves. I had to change the towels every 5–10 minutes because they would become steaming hot. I had no fever.

I was sure I had gotten muscular and nerve inflammations and was terrified. I thought it must be really serious, so I didn't dare to go to the doctor because they had misdiagnosed me and/or scared me at other times. So I only went after some weeks when the worst of the sensation of burning was over. They said since I did not have any neurological dysfunction, the nerves and the tissue would probably heal by itself, and they agreed that it was muscular and nerve inflammation from over-exercise. Four years later, I still have some left.

It took me about two months to start to function, still like a sick person with a very low capacity, but at least not in bed all the time. It has since been a process of healing, little by little regaining my health and my energy. I have thought about the symptoms after the experience as muscular and nerve inflammation. I also thought the symptoms were connected to the illness before the ritual and over-practicing physical yoga.

It wasn't until 2021 when I read Gopi Krishna's account of his Kundalini experience that I started to think differently. Of course, I had thought about what had happened in the ritual as related to Kundalini. I was practicing the traditions of Tantra and Hatha Yoga and was quite informed by then. But this extreme physical sensation of burning up wasn't something I felt I could ascribe to Kundalini. It just seemed too physical.

This understanding that an experience this physical must have been brought on by something equally physical changed when I understood that Gopi Krishna (author of *Living with Kundalini*) also had had the experience of burning up, even though he did not have a physical practice but only a seated visual meditation practice.

Gopi Krishna understood the heat as Kundalini having gone up the wrong (right, Pingala) channel. I have heard about this understanding before but as I understand the tantric tradition, that developed the concept of Kundalini, it cannot enter any other channel than the central channel (Shushumna).

It seems to me from my experience that Kundalini is a spiritual fire, consuming and then rebuilding the system.

All the yogic traditions talk about tapas; an inner heat, that the practice is supposed to build up.

Tantric yogic tradition connects tapas to the power of the will and to the life force. Will and life force as desire are personified by the goddess Tripurasundari who is connected to Shushumna. The fire of Kundalini is said to ascend through the Shushumna (the central energy channel).

After understanding Kundalini as a spiritual fire, the dream after the angel initiations started to make sense. 'The fire will consume what is needed bit by bit as you meet it.'

A month or two after the ritual, I asked inside why this was happening to me. It all seemed too much to handle, especially with small children who needed me. It felt like a really harsh punishment. When I asked inside I "heard," "You are going to be a messenger."

I didn't believe what I heard. It sounded pretentious, and I thought it came from my mind. I asked for some other form of communication, not happening through my thoughts. The morning after, when I woke up, there was a dove on my lawn. It came to live on my lawn acting as a dog for two days. It wouldn't leave so I brought it water, which it took. After two days, I looked up the symbology of the dove and it said 'messenger'; after that, the dove left.

Being Rebuilt

During the 'healing', years that followed, I had a lot of what I thought of as cleansing being done on my head. Earwax clogged my ears for weeks at a time. My eyelids and area around the eyes swelled up and became red and dry for weeks at a time. I had to keep them constantly smeared with fat since the skin just absorbed it and demanded more.

In the summer of 2019, I was in a retreat with the tantric teacher. I was there to assist my healing.

During the retreat, a yellow light flooded into my eyes during an interaction with another person at the retreat. It happened as I had become confused over having misread the personality of the person. In the light, the person's face started to shift to different ages, cultures and genders. Every face had a different quality that I hadn't been able to read from the person, but that became clear as I saw these faces.

I remember I had the same ability in my early twenties but not on the same scale, and at that time I did not really understand what I saw.

The person in question also got the yellow light flooding that person's vision experiencing being shown who the person could become.

In the autumn of 2019, I dreamt that I was getting treatment from a girl at the tantric teacher's request. The treatment was that she smoked something and then blew the smoke into my face for maybe an hour. The experience was very physical. I could feel the smell of the smoke. I got nauseated by having to breathe in the smoke for such a long time. When she was finished, I thought that nothing had happened. But then I discovered enormous amounts of waste products having been excavated from my ears, my eyes, my nose and my mouth.

The tantric teacher told me that the treatment exists and is called Dhumapan, which is an Ayurvedic treatment to clear the openings of the head from waste products; ama.

During these years, I felt psychologically like I was getting purged of false notions. What I had experienced before as demands of perfection from Christ was now experienced simply as seeing clearly and accepting the truth.

As part of this, I started to experience my life story, and others as a continuation of a learning process reaching over several lives; a notion I had never been able to embrace before.

Mantra repetition that had such an effect before didn't seem to 'hit' any resistance or increase the vibration in the body as before. The vibration in the body seemed to be at maximum speed all the time.

In the autumn of 2019, I started to get reports of yellow/golden light from my yoga students. It had happened a little the years before but not at all on this scale.

Here are some of the experiences of the students. I had never talked to them about yellow or golden light:

"Yesterday a lot of yellow light. It was like lightning streaks from different directions in the room."

"This Friday when you pressed on me in Adho Mukha Svanasana… All the sounds got centered around us and the volume went up… This time there was resistance in me and I couldn't quite let it go. But my inner space was filled with a strong yellow light followed by insights about old traumas and blockages… In Shavasana, my chest and heart ached and then released to leave so much more space."

"…as the day when you showed the flow of Warrior 2… I can't explain, it hit me right in the heart, I was so overwhelmed. The next day…my subconscious painted Warrior 2 in strong colors of gold and copper (I never use gold, copper or silver when I paint but that day it was those colors that kept on coming.)"

There were other experiences of energy reported as well. Experiences of energy moving inside the body forcefully, experiences of vast space, experiences of having been 'held' through life and/or being loved through life, experiences of the heart area opening up or overflowing, subconscious memory surfacing, experiences of shaking, energy rushing up through the center of the body/spine, the body taking over the movement, sometimes creating very fast movements resulting in shaking and an experience of very intense energy taking

163

over, hearing me talk to them as if I stood close to them and then discovering that I was far away from them in the room, a feeling of the top of the head opening up.

None of the students related their experiences directly to me. Many related their experiences to their own contact with the divine, to the group or to the room that the classes were held in.

The Calling

At the beginning of January 2020, my family and I went to France. It was on the French Riviera.

One day, we decided to visit an old village in the mountains, Gourdon. It was medieval. I had a feeling I wanted to enter the chapel there, so I did.

There was a wooden statue in the back of the small chapel. The statue I think was a depiction of Mary since the chapel was Mary's chapel. I felt drawn to it. When I stopped in front of it, I heard in my thoughts from the statue. 'I will make you great. You will do my work.'

After this, the process of seeing clearly continued, confronting me with the extent of falseness and egotism of humans. This continued for several years.

In the spring of 2021, I dreamt that I was shown that all the years that I thought I would meet the Goddess (creation), I met Shiva (dissolution). It was the year 2012 and 2018 and one more year I couldn't clearly remember when waking up (maybe 2020). These were years when I had a feeling something big was about to happen and a feeling of excitement, but then what had happened had been all but pleasant. Now though it seemed as if it was time to meet the Goddess.

I was to ride on a male goat. It smelled goat (doesn't usually bother me) but the feeling was a bit too physical in a bad way. I didn't want to and tried to get away by claiming that I couldn't get up on it. Then the goat got down on its stomach with its legs out to the sides so that I just had to step over it. I checked up on the symbolic connection between the goddess and the male goat. I found that the male goat symbolises the ego and that riding it symbolises mastering it, in the Indian goddess tradition.

During Navaratri (festival for the Goddess) in the evening (20/5) that spring, I felt an extreme energy in the body, the activity so high. When I went to bed, I had a feeling of tingling in my nerves at the bottom of my spine and then a feeling like a paintbrush painting with a stroke over the spine up to the top of my head, where there was a soft release. I then saw colors of yellow and white light. Since Saraswati is connected to white and yellow, I thought of her. Then I saw a transparent picture of a Chinese-looking goddess. Later I thought that might have been Tara. I saw the picture of the goddess projected onto an internal image of myself lying in the bed. The image stayed for what seemed like a long time until I registered that the goddess had placed her ring, having a subtle white flame on top, at the placement of my Spiritual Eye. I then 'heard' her saying: 'Now you see it all.'

There is a mystical passage in the Bible that might refer to the Spiritual Eye. The tantric yogic tradition calls the Spiritual Eye; Ajna. There is said to reside a subtle white flame here called Itara linga.

Matthew 6:22, King James Version

The light of the body is the eye: if therefore thine eye be single, thy whole body shall be full of light.

The word single (haplous) indicates what is united and undivided.

After this, I felt as if being pulled down into unconsciousness. I felt the same group of beings, whose presence I have felt many times before, working on me.

There was transparent liquid light with colors floating inside. It seemed as if they were using this to work on me. I tried to keep conscious but at some point, I lost consciousness.

The day after, sometime during the day, I remembered what had followed in a flash. They had finished with me after having dug a hole in my chest. My body was made of something that looked like clay. They finished by putting a perfect smoke-colored crystal heart in my chest and then closed it. While putting it down they said: 'Together in love'. It meant me and the divine united in love. I got a feeling that they were finished with me. A feeling of completion. Of what I didn't know.

I looked up the symbology of smokey crystal (quartz). I found it explained as a crystal traditionally used by shamans and druids, connecting heaven and earth.

In the summer of 2021, I learned that Mary, the mother of Christ, was viewed as the ultimate mystic since she connected heaven and earth by giving birth to Christ. I connected this to my experience of Mary telling me that I would do her work.

The shamans, the rishis, the prophets, the druids, and the mystics are all seen as messengers between the worlds.

Message

Well, I guess a messenger needs to have a message.

If I have learned anything it is this:

There is a law or an order above the laws of the transient world.

That law or order is that of truth. It is eternal and unchanging.

Truth as we perceive it is a fire that burns what is untrue and lights up and gives clarity.

Truth is also life, even eternal life, as opposed to death. We can understand this by using the concept of Prana in the yogic tradition as life force or animating principle, also the Hebrew word ruach refers to the animating principle of God. Both of these concepts are associated with wind. The Spirit as wind is also found in the New Testament.

John 3:8

The wind blows wherever it pleases. You hear its sound, but you cannot tell where it comes from or where it is going. So it is with everyone born of the Spirit."

Truth is not transient but unchanging and only the transient dissolves at some point.

The higher order of truth is described as light, life and unity. This is described by Christ as well as the non-dual tantric tradition.

The underlying truth is not different from the reality we perceive, it's just a deeper experience and understanding of the same.

It seems from these traditions that our lives are constantly created out of the consequences of our actions. We are constantly creating our lives by our actions.

It also seems as if repentance and changing our ways can alter our lives, and debts can be written off.

Consequence can be understood to be part of the truth as its results point back to the underlying truth, giving us a lesson or a deeper understanding.

It seems that if our wishes are not in alignment with truth and life, all we will manifest will be untruth and death.

We live and we learn, probably through many lifetimes.

We cannot take over anybody else's lesson, and no one can take over ours.

Since the truth cannot be avoided forever, everyone will find it.

Matthew 7:7–8

"Ask and it will be given to you; seek and you will find; knock and the door will be opened to you. For everyone who asks receives; the one who seeks finds; and to the one who knocks, the door will be opened.

It is not a mystery. It is here for anyone who wants to receive it.

For whoever has ears.

Epilogue

22 September 2023

As we have seen the word 'kamala' is used to refer to the union of Shiva and Shakti; as the light radiance of their union. Shiva is sometimes referred to as white bindu and Shakti is sometimes referred to as red bindu in their forms as Kameshwari and Kameshwara. The mixture of these is referred to as a color of rosy red. The goddess Kamala through her association with the Vedic goddess Lakshmi is connected to the colors gold and rosy red. At the end of the Kundalini process, in her liberated state, Kamala may be viewed as the transcendence of the world, expressing itself in the world, reforming it.

From the end of spring 2023, a color of rosy red started to fill my inner vision and head on different occasions. The color lemon yellow also started to come with the rosy red color in dreams and visions.

After this, an old memory from when I was 20 years old came back of an especially vivid 'dream' where a parachute in that color (rosy red) fell from the sky over me. The feeling in the dream was utter awe and complete overwhelm.

Before this color started to fill my head in 2023, there had been a long period of time starting during 2021 where I would

171

wake up during the night with the inner vision of having golden dust falling inside my body. First in the throat, then in my physical eyes and then from the top of my head down through my head.

As we have seen, the Kundalini process is a downward trajectory into creation, an upward trajectory into liberation and a downward trajectory as an expression of that liberation.

The Hatha Yoga tradition that succeeded the tantric tradition lost track of this and mainly focused on the upward trajectory. This probably happened because of a return to earlier shramana philosophy with the ideal of transcendence and not immanence.

We have also seen in the stories of Buddha and Christ that they are going beyond the power of the representations of temporal fulfilment and death; the devil and Mara. But as they do this, it is not happening solely in some other realm but influencing the material world. They also chose to spread their message in the material world.

Bibliography

Books

Aurobindo, Sri
The Mother
Pondicherry, Sri Aurobindo Ashram Trust, 1995

Bodo, Murray
10 Christian Mystics and what They Tell Us of God
Audiobook, Now You Know Media Inc, 2008

Chinnaiyan, Kavitha M.
Shakti Rising:
Embracing Shadow and Light on the Goddess Path to
Wholeness.
Oakland, New Harbinger Publications, Inc, 2017

Goswami, Shyam Sundar
Layayoga
The Definitive Guide to the Chakras and Kundalini
Rochester, Inner Traditions International, 1999

Commentary by Joo, Swami Lakshman
Vijnana Bhairava

173

The Practice of Centering Awereness
Varanasi, Indica Books, 1995

Kempton, Sally
Awakening Shakti
The Transformative Power of the Goddesses of Yoga
Boulder, Sounds True Inc, 2013

Kinsley, David
Tantric Visions of the Divine Feminine
The Ten Mahavidyas
London, University of California Press, Ltd, 1997

Kinsley, David R.
Hindu Goddesses
Visions of the Divine Feminine in the Hindu Religious Tradition
London, University of California Press, Ltd, 1986

Saraswati, Swami Satyananda
Asana Pranayama Mudra Bandha
Munger, Bihar School of Yoga, 1996

Saraswati, Swami Satyananda
Kundalini Tantra
Munger, Yoga Publications Trust, 1984

Saraswati, Swami Satyananda
A Systematic Course in the Ancient Tantric Techniques of Yoga and Kriya
Munger, Yoga Publications Trust, 1981

174

Silburn, Lilian
Kundalini
The energy of the Depths
Albany, State University of New York Press, 1988

Wallis, Christopher D.
Tantra illuminated
The Philosophy, History, and Practice of a Timeless Tradition
Petaluma, Mattamayura Press, 2013

Documentary Film/Filmed lectures

Eakins; Pamela
Innanas Descent
Terra Nova Seminary
Accessed on YouTube March 1-2024

Grubin, David
The Buddha:
The Story of Siddhartha
PBS Documentary Film, 2010
Accessed on YouTube March 1-2024

Kempton, Sally
Kundalini
Teleclass, 2016

Mallinson, James
James Mallinson on "Tantric Traditions and Hathayoga"
Brown University. Lecture March 12, 2019 at Brown University
Accessed on YouTube March 1-2024

Pagels, Elaine
What do "secret gospels" suggest about Jesus and his teaching?
Kaufman Interfaith Institute. Lecture 30/10-2019, Annual Interfaith Academic Conference
Accessed on YouTube March 1-2024

Pagels, Elaine
St. Lukes Atlanta. Lecture March 7, 2020, Part 1
Accessed on YouTube March 1-2024

Sarvapriyananda, Swami & Tamalsina, Staneshwar
Vedanta and Tantra Kashmir Shaivism/ A Dialog between Philosophies
Vivekananda Samiti, IIT Kanpur
Accessed on YouTube March 1-2024

Thurman, Robert A.F.
The Tibetan path of enlightenment
Media Factory, Pathways to the Spirit lecture, October 23,1998
Accessed on YouTube March 1-2024

Thurman, Robert A.F.
How is Buddhist Vajrayana a Force For Good?
Buddhism explained with Robert A.F. Thurman
Tibet House US Menla Online. Lecture 9/11 2016, Tibet House US
Accessed on YouTube March 1-2024

Tompkins, Christopher
Patreon Q & A Session-Kundalini: Everything you've been wanting to know
Christopher Tompkins
Accessed on YouTube March 1-2024

Wallis, Christopher D.
What is the original Kundalini Yoga?
Christopher Wallis,
Accessed on Youtube March 1-2024

Wallis, Christopher D.
What is Kundalini?
Christopher Wallis
Accessed on YouTube March 1-2024

Websites

Access to Insight
Translation by Bhikku, Thanissaro
Ayacana Sutta: The request
https://www.accesstoinsight.org
Accessed on March 1-2024

Biblegateway
Bible: New International Version. King James Version. New American Bible (Revised Edition). New Revised Standard Version (Updated Edition). Young's Literal Translation.
https://www.biblegateway.com
Accessed on March 1-2024

Brittanica
https://www.brittanica.com
Accessed on March 1-2024

Buddhanet
https://www.buddhanet.net
Accessed on March 1-2024

Gnosis
Translation by Grant, Robert M.
The Gospel of Truth
http://gnosis.org
Accessed on March 1-2024

Gnosis
Translation by Isenberg, Wesley W.
Gospel of Philip
http://gnosis.org
Accessed on March 1-2024

Marquette
Translation by Lambdin, Thomas O.
Gospel of Thomas
https://www.marquette.edu
Accessed on March 1-2024

Ions
https://noetic.org
Accessed on March 1-2024

Wikipedia
https://en.m.wikipedia.org
Accessed on March 1-2024

Yogananda Self Realization Fellowship Blog
https://yogananda.org
Accessed on March 1-2024